"ADVENTURE TRAVEL"

A NEW PARTNERSHIP

THE ROYAL PRINCESS

Mark J. Curran

Order this book online at www.trafford.com
or email orders@trafford.com

Most Trafford titles are also available at major online book retailers.

Print information available on the last page.

ISBN: 978-1-6987-1623-7 (sc)
ISBN: 978-1-6987-1622-0 (e)

Trafford rev. 01/04/2024

North America & international
toll-free: 844-688-6899 (USA & Canada)
fax: 812 355 4082

Mike and Amy and the Royal Princess

PREFACE

AN EXPLANATION[1]

This is the 6th in the series of "Adventure Travel" stories, originally based on the author's three staff assignments on expedition trips on the National Geographic Explorer for Lindblad Expeditions. The new series would be fiction with main characters Michael Gaherty and Amy Carrier on trips to Brazil (1972), Mexico (1974), Spain and Portugal (1976), Guatemala (1980) and Colombia (1982).

The years have passed; it is now 1989, Mike and Amy are still great friends, some – time lovers, and work partners on past AT trips. Mike is a Full Professor at the University of Nebraska in Spanish, Portuguese, and Latin American Studies. He has not worked for AT since 1982 and Colombia. Amy continues with AT. She handles ship and shore logistics (lodging, shore outings). If the Partnership proposal is approved, Mike will handle cultural introductions on ship and accompany on shore excursions with guides. Both Mike and Amy are now in their 40s, but in the prime of life. The Partnership (nicknamed by soon to be Arkansas Royal Princess friends as the "Float Trip") is an entirely new concept and requires an explanation. The itinerary, to be seen shortly, is new to Mike and his

---

[1] Author's statement: as I write this in 2023 and refer to all those real time events of 1989, the entire region and many countries and cities are in trouble – from local politics to actual bloody conflict. Example one: Russia, the Ukraine and Crimea (Odessa in our case). Although we did not visit Israel or Palestine, we were not far from them, and strife is always potentially present in Cyprus, Crete and in today's Dubrovnik. In both real-life travel in 1989 and our account in fiction, Adventure Travel and Royal Princess were fortunate.

expertise in the area to be seen is limited to study and research and without in − country experience. Amy, on the other hand, even though the itinerary is new, can handle her usual duties, working with Royal Princess personnel.

All this for now is in Mike's head and it's like a bill in congress − he has to sell it to Adventure Travel and get the votes to approve it. If it all works, here is the plan for the Partnership. Times have changed; AT continues its usual expeditions based mostly on flora, fauna and nature, but this is a sharp departure from that. AT would partner with a major cruise − travel company, Royal Princess Lines, to do a joint venture. The aim is to travel to the most important cities and sites of the Eastern Mediterranean, experience these places and their history. Mike would lecture on the places but would need serious help from local guides and experts. Amy would coordinate on − ship with Princess, but both would be liaison with AT "Adventurers" along for the ride.

I

MEETING AMY

I had envisioned the trip for early Fall in 1989, incidentally, good weather in the Mediterranean region, so I got the ball rolling with a call to Amy via the AT office in Los Angeles. It was March 1989, ugly weather in Nebraska, temperatures hovering just above zero, some snow, some sleet, some rain, Nebraska's "springtime," typical for the time. The only good thing, the one million Sand Hill Cranes out on the Platte were cackling, jumping up and down in mating dances, recently arrived from the usual warmer climes of Bosque del Apache in New Mexico and the lakes and ponds around Wilcox in Arizona, "snowbirds" as it were. Spring break in another week would bring that other "migration," U of N students and faculty fleeing anywhere for a warm weather break. So, it is a good time to connect with Amy.

Susan Gilliam the second in charge to James Morrison, the CEO of AT, informed me that Amy was on duty on the "International Explorer" but due to dock in Los Angeles this weekend. She used her "pull" to connect me land to ship and I heard that marvelous voice once again. We did the usual chit-chat for five minutes before I sprang my "brainstorm" of a new trip. Amy was used to this "drill," and said, "Ole' boy, things must be getting pretty boring in Lincoln. I really expected to hear from you much sooner, as in years. Geeze, it's only been seven years! Oh, I get it, the 'seven-year itch,' but not with me, ahem, maybe another woman. You must be horny. Hey, that's not all bad. My god, we are both turned 40. Is everything still in working order?"

This was pretty salty talk coming from the ship to shore line (not always private!) So what! Not much to lose now. "Yes, you have surmised correctly, but that is another matter. I want to talk about work and a trip that will knock your socks off, and perhaps one that would lead to another chapter in our (choose one only) steamy - lukewarm - icy relationship. (We both did laugh.) Are you dyeing your hair yet? And I can only assume ship and shore have that luscious body in fine fettle! That's a compliment. Whoa. I'm getting off the subject. Would you be willing for me to meet you in Los Angeles when the 'International Adventurer' docks, share a weekend with me and I'll propose again. No, not getting hooked. That didn't work out very well last time. I mean, a rough sketch of my dream trip. If you like it, we're right in town and can go see James Morrison at AT. At worst, we can catch up, check each other out and maybe move on to more interesting things."

"Mike, just to tell you, there's a lot of water under that bridge, some maybe a bit unpleasant for you, but you've caught me in, uh, hiatus, so yes, it's a date. Why don't you meet me at the ship when it docks in San Pedro this coming Saturday, reintroduce yourself to all the old friends (I mean the crew, most of whom are still hanging around), we can have a great lunch on board and then off to hotel land."

I was relieved to hear what I just heard. "It's a deal; tell Captain Tony and Chef Romano I'm a'coming."

"Oh, this will have to be after we have all the Adventurers safely off to the four corners of the world. Probably 2 p.m."

"Fine, I'll make reservations for the Marriott (your old-time employer) in Westwood and we'll have a place to lay our heads and weary bones."

"They still have separate queens, right? Do that."

Now, inquisitive reader, I had already checked out Princess Cruise's fall schedule and after dry-dock in late August for two weeks, it would be available for a fall expedition, destinations already on its calendar.

II

SATURDAY ON THE "INTERNATIONAL ADVENTURER"

I got that shuttle bus ride from Lincoln to Omaha and a United flight to Los Angeles on that Saturday morning and an expensive taxi ride to the San Pedro harbor. There it was in front of my eyes – a sore sight to see – the "Adventurer." Upon closer inspection on the quay, it seemed in fine shape (even though seven years older), a brilliant white paint job, flags flying, and after being granted permission to board, old friend Exec Officer Martim Mendes at the top of the stairway to greet me. I said, "Permissão a subir a bordo, Oficial Mendes?"

"O' arretado, você não precisa de formalidades. Bem vindo a bordo!"

As I walked up the steps, we sized each other up. Seven years! Yes, there were changes, me a little heavier and with less hair, he fit as a fiddle but graying hair at the temples. Our short conversation was in Portuguese (he the continental from Lisboa, me the "colonial" from Rio). He said the "special luncheon" would be in the Chart Deck room and there were some old friends already there to greet me. Indeed! Captain Tony, Harry Downing (still around having come back from "retirement,") Chef Romano awaiting with the goodies, and this beautiful woman, still in ship attire, but beaming with a huge smile and a warm kiss applauded by all. Everyone all had questions at once, but with fine Vinho Verde in the glasses, we all had a wonderful, initial renewal of friendship.

They all wondered how life was in the "sertão," the great American outback, joked about not expecting a long answer, and lamented my seven-year absence. I just hinted briefly there was a plan in the works for a return, but too early to confirm. No need to repeat all the chatter that took place, but Captain Tony reckoned "Adventurer" had done 100 trips I missed out on! I sat by him, Amy at his side, and Exec Martin and Harry across the table. The former apologized more staff were not present, but "Adventurer" was already deep in the process of cleaning and welcoming a new batch of adventurers that evening, destination, the west coast of South America, around the Horn, and angling up the Atlantic to Lisbon for major refitting.

Amy was on temporary shore leave before joining them once again in Lisbon, then south to the Cape and over to India. Wow. But it was small talk, lots of laughter, reminiscing of the last big trip to Portugal and Spain and its dicey times, good Lord, more than ten years ago. (Amy and my trips to Guatemala and Colombia were of course more recent but did not involve "Adventurer.") She would disembark with me; we would go to the Marriot for that "reunion" and then attend to business at AT in Los Angeles.

Chef Romano apologized he could not provide the big spread of a fine dinner on board, but humbly offered four courses, calamari and grilled shrimp appetizer, green salad, a special lasagna recipe ("I prepared this for the Pope"), and in my honor that chocolate − coconut dessert I raved about years earlier. We switched to generous glasses of Chianti, and wonderful demitasse "bicas" (Portugal's answer to Brazil's "cafezinhos") later. By this time, it was almost four p.m. and Captain Antônio excused himself. I raved about the luncheon and said I would hopefully have some news soon for a real reunion. Curiosity abounded, but sealed lips was the call.

Amy went to her room up on the captain's deck and quarters, returned with a large backpack she allowed me to carry ("Just like old disembarkation huh?") and we grabbed a taxi to the Marriott. Heavy Los Angeles traffic ensued, but the driver was an expert at dodging the zealous "angeleños" and we were delivered by 5:00 check – in.

III

AT THE MARRIOT

In our spacious room, uh, with those two queen beds, but with a divan and easy chairs, we basically sat at each end of the divan, sized each other up with pithy comments as how "We had hardly changed at all" (Ha! And laughter). I have not said that we had kept in touch, off and on, since 1982. We recalled Guatemala and Colombia with great relish. To make a long story short (since this book will be a very long story), we got down to brass tacks, Amy went first. Her first love was and still is indeed AT and the ship and all the travel, all over the world several times. She had three (I surmised, at least) serious friendships on board and off board during the seven years. "Sometimes wonderful, sometimes not so wonderful, but not regretted." There were two offers of marriage, but like with me in the past, not accepted. She wanted the attention, the romance, the camaraderie, but not the invitation to be "tied down." Hmm. So, nothing had changed in that regard.

"So, how about you? Is there more to say than the phone conversations, yes, and occasional letters?"

"Amy, I wish, I wish. Not for not wanting. But you are the closest I ever came to a real bonding for life. And I am not over the decision (yours more than mine) of nixing marriage a few years ago. I guess my Mom and Dad back in Nebraska are still waiting for their youngest son to 'settle down.' But Amy, with whom? Like you, or maybe not, there were two or three

I guess you could call it affairs, with good looking Latina ladies from the U. Good times, but never quite right. So, you find me now in my 40s and wondering if time has passed me by."

"Michael, I assure you, even with this brief renewal, that that has not happened. You are 'aging well.' (Ha ha). I'm sorry; I forget details, sometimes cannot get it straight, but I believe teaching, researching and writing have gone well. You are after all, now, a Full Professor! And I understand about those Latinas; you always did have a wandering eye for them! But now, the difficult part, uh, how is your wandering eye doing looking at the also 'Casa dos 40' ['In her 40s'] Amy Carrier? I can tell you because you will get it, it has not been easy to keep mind and especially body up to standards. I work out like crazy on the ships, have kept my weight close to that of seven years ago, but the "violão" shape has changed a bit. The important part, pardon me, upper body, is still nice, but with a little more support needed, but the "xoxota" (as you liked to tease me) is in fine shape. I'll see if we can find a time to see about all that. It's also mental and the bullshit stress of TV ads and the times reminding me I'm not 22 anymore. But you know, you and I both have our own minds about all that. Enough already. Tell me about the "brainstorm" and see if it all adds up. Then, uh, we can socialize.

So here is what I told Amy, noting right now it is all very tentative. "Prior to the trip, we will have to convince AT's CEO, James Morrison, that it is all viable. Amy, here is my plan:"

THE MEDITERRANEAN – A VOYAGE IN HISTORY

The itinerary already planned by Princess Cruises will loosely follow Classic Literature of the Greeks and Romans and their narrative structure: "10 Cantos" (or chapters) of the "Iliad," the "Odyssey" and the "Aeneid."

Canto I. Rome

Canto II. Venice

Canto III. Dubrovnik

Canto IV. (Knossos) Heraklion, Crete

Canto V. Ephesus inland from Izmir Turkey

Canto VI. Istanbul

Canto VII. Russia - Yalta and Odessa

Canto VIII. The Bosphorus Strait, the Black Sea and On Board the Princess

Canto IX. Greece - The Greek Islands: Delos and Mykonos

Canto X. Greece -Athens and Sounion

Denouement: The Last Days, Naples and Home

"The trip will be a very full three weeks in the Fall of 1989, coming up shortly. I've done my homework. Note that this now is a peaceful time in the region. The end of the 30 - year Cold War has come with the Malta Conference, Eastern Bloc countries have declared independence from Russia, and the Berlin Wall is coming down. It is a good time to travel, serendipity rules. I can fill you in with all the details of the itinerary. The trip is very ambitious. The kicker is to approve and set up the Partnership – AT and Princess Lines, but it can be done. It will be nothing like AT has done before. I will have my ducks in a row with the cultural – history introductions. AT's partner, Princess Cruise Lines, will handle most on-shore logistics. I've already unofficially checked with them and they say it is all feasible and 'a piece of cake.' Your job will be coordinating with them, but hey, I think you will have a lot more freedom to be with me at these incredible places."

Then came Amy's response:

"At first glance, it seems too ambitious, way too ambitious. But just like you. After all, you arranged the deal with New York Times Travel a few years ago, and that turned out great for them and AT. Secondly, it is a total departure from AT philosophy and culture – honey babe, we don't do current and ancient history except as minimal prep for our normal itineraries. YOU are the one who will have to convince James."

"Amy, the whole itinerary is already set and planned and being promoted by Princess. What we are doing is 'sweetening the pie' for them with our Adventurers. AT is just really adding significantly to the passenger list. As the Royal Princess goes, it is much larger, much more elegant, much more comfortable than the "International Adventurer" (Sorry). Another world. I know the ship is a whopping change, but change is a good thing, right? (I showed Amy photos and a brochure of the ship from a past trip.) I'm also thinking, ahem, you and I can have the 'honeymoon' trip we missed out on a while back. So, let's reacquaint ourselves a bit and chew this one over."

She rolled her eyes (in a joking way) and said, "Mike, it's déjà vu all over again. We've been through this a time or two before. You have the Irish Blarney, and those places will even fill in a lot of blanks for me. AT would not go there otherwise. Let's sleep on it."

Curious reader, that is what we did. I ordered two bottles of champagne from room service and we did Marriott's "fine dining" with Amy in charge of choosing the eats in the top floor restaurant. Familiar readers (I know who you are) will recognize the menu choices indicated by Amy. Oh, one thing, gulp, I had to pay the bill. James Morrison did, later, reimburse me, but not without saying, "You caught me off guard on this one Gaherty!"

That night we used only one queen bed. Both of us had forgotten how comfortable we were with each other in many such times in the past. Uh oh. I was falling in love again. Amy did manage to say, "I always loved you, Gaherty. We match well. Career got in the way. Tonight, however is fun. Can we leave it at that? You know, a raincheck on serious talk."

"All right, all right, but only if you say you are at least open to a, uh, frank discussion on the topic, time and place to be determined."

It was like JACK BENNY on the old radio show when he was accosted by a robber: "Your money or your life." "I'M THINKING … I'M THINKING." Finally, …

"… Agreed, now let's check things all out again."

"Whew."

IV

WITH JAMES MORRISON

That next a.m. over an early light breakfast, I gave Amy more details, doing my Rotarian best to share the cultural and other possibilities of the trip. It must have worked because she said we should call James for an appointment that afternoon and Mike Gaherty would be on the hook to make the sale. We were set for 3:00 p.m. and I had to put on the old thinking cap and prep for the meeting.

We got priority over other demands and James said he would look forward to seeing us, all old friends. It was old hat to readers, routine much the same. Susan Gilliam, second in charge, greeted us, gave a big hug to Amy and a careful one to me, served good coffee and we were getting caught up when the phone buzzed and James came down the hallway to greet us. Like us (and for me in the absence), he was a bit older, but not the least changed in demeanor or efficiency. Still the 'granny glasses.' He lamented my absence from AT, smiled, and wondered if I had to clean the hayseed out of my ears from Lincoln. Ha ha. "And my friend, in case I didn't know, what brings you here? The rest of the afternoon is clear so no hurry, and maybe that dinner at Chasen's later? We've been saving up for it."

With brochures, photos and lots of planning I spilled the beans. "James, you know, uh, I come up with new ideas for AT now and again. You recall the New York Times Travel suggestions. I think you know that went well, heh, heh. I've got another one but maybe more adventurous and surer to get your attention."

I presented my plan, already known to the reader via talk with Amy, but in more detail: creating a partnership with Princess Cruise Lines for a joint venture, albeit a vast departure from AT tradition. Joint travel on the Royal Princess in late September of 1989 for a spectacular overview of the major cities in the Middle and Eastern Mediterranean, their respective histories and cultures and Princess treatment for AT Adventurers. James, no dummy with his head stuck in the sand, knew all about Princess Lines. His first reaction, a shaking of the head meaning "no way," saying, "Gaherty what have you been smoking lately. I hear it grows wild along the Platte in Nebraska."

"Just us farmers' rolled corn husk reefers, James (laugh). Give me fifteen minutes to go into the details." He said, "You can have until hell freezes over on this one for all the good it will do you. I think there's a round file here we can deposit all that pile of propaganda you're trying to shovel off on me (a reference to one of Nebraska's rural products). Go ahead."

I had the Princess itinerary already shown to Amy. My plan if James agreed: we would need to get the price list for passengers, and James needed to get on the phone to negotiate what they would offer to AT for its own prospective travelers (i.e., possible discounts to help fill the ship) plus fees for Amy and my services, and advertising. It would all have to be post haste. This is March and advertising would have to be done by May so the final trip brochure would be available to prospective travelers. James was thoughtful as usual (I could see the wheels turning in that brain).

He offered, "Times are evolving. There is more and more competition for the nature trips, and honestly, less nature. We just have to work harder to find it, find the animals' schedules and plan accordingly. Cousteau has his own trips and is pretty tight with sharing with others. Lindblad Expeditions and National Geographic are in expansion mode. And there is a dozen more companies out there. Adventurers have always been open to history and culture, true, secondary to the nature, but maybe this would be a 'sell.' Mike, you are walking the plank for this one, and it's a short plank. I figure we would have to round up 100 paying passengers, but the Royal Princess has a capacity for 800. I'll commit to taking the first steps and see what happens."

He smiled, we shook hands, and that evening repeated a wonderful dinner at Chasens with all those old movie star posters on the walls (W.C. Fields, Mae West, Jack Benny, Clark Gable, Marilyn Monroe, and John Wayne and Paul Newman among the latest). Drinks, good wine with a dinner pleasing even to fancy cuisine Amy ensued. From then on, it was two months of a flurry of activity, seen below.

Princess's CEO Joe Caufield and James sparred with each other, made offers and counter offers, but came to an agreement the following week. After that it all came fast and furious. A beautiful, colorful trip brochure with equal credits to Princess and AT was ready by May with all the usual attractions and small print. (Trip insurance among them; it could cost many thousands of dollars to be air lifted to a hospital in case of dire emergency.) In this case it was not the crew, the staff or even the speakers that were highlighted; it was the Royal Princess itself, the amazing itinerary and blurbs on each place. At first glance, overwhelming, it was billed as a "Mediterranean Odyssey – A Trip into History."

The response was overwhelming! AT got its 100 people by July and Princess Cruises its 700 by August. Many repeat Adventurers signed up, most all known to Amy and many to me. Accommodations were all first – class and Adventurers could reserve tables in fine dining most evenings. The RP team would handle everything else. Amy would coordinate with on – board ship and shore people and I would prepare the on – board introductions to the places we would visit. I spent three solid months boning up, preparing notes and short talks, the most challenging task I had ever had, far more than the academic research on Latin America in the sense of time frame. James was happy, wished us well and said he would be waiting for reports. So, it began.

CANTO I

ROME

Amy and I and a few old - timers from former AT trips boarded TWA in New York for the red eye all night direct flight to Rome where we would be booked by Princess at the Ambasciatore Hotel (a fine start). I might note we were packed in a full flight, doing our version of sardines in a can. Oh well. Surely things would get better, and they did. Princess was efficient at Rome's huge Leonardo da Vinci International Airport, got us on a bus to Villa Burghese and the "old money" Ambassador. Amy and I were of course "roomies" and after an efficient check - in had an egg omelet breakfast (I noted the regular price, $35 USD) but the tariff already included in the trip. We tried to nap, but only succeeded in one hour. I changed money at the hotel, $125 USD for 175,000 lire. (I will have to get used to the local currency; it can slip through your fingers.)

We were on our own the rest of that first day, and uh, overdid it. It was a bit of a blur: the Via Veneto and then Piazza Barberini on the Quirinal Hill. We saw our first Roman fountain (uh, more to come). I will try to note all this, give short blurbs on what we will see, but don't know how long this will last.

The entire piazza was owned by the Barberini family, Pope Urban one of them. He commissioned Bernini (we will get to know him more later) to do the Triton Fountain. Triton, a minor sea god, is drinking from a conch and four dolphins support him. Wow.

The Triton Fountain, Rome

Then came another astounding Roman scene – the Piazza Colonna and Marcus Aurelius' Column, another of empire days' construction. We would learn it was a custom for the emperors responsible for enlarging the empire to record it all, uh, not in writing, but in a carved stone column depicting not in a humble way, all phases of battles. Amy said "It's like the skyscrapers in New York, bigger and better." It won't be the last, and supposedly is based on an even more famous one called Trajan's Column we would see later. Here's the "dope" on it and my photo.

Trajan's circus and column and Church of the Holy Name of Mary behind it. He was the best of the Antonine emperors, year 113 A.D. He used the spoils of the Dacian campaign (now Romania) to build his forum. When Emperor Constantine of Constantinople, first Christian emperor, visited Rome in 356 A.D. he was astounded by the beauty of the place.

The column itself was done by Apollodorus of Damascus, Syria. It is 125 feet high with seventeen marble drums, each sculpted in spirals depicting episodes in Trajan's war against the Dacians. There are over one hundred scenes; it would be 656 feet long if rolled out flat: it is a faithful historic account of the Dacian war and Roman military technique. (A nearby tourist was heard to whisper "Who Cares?") The statue of St. Peter on its top today (since 1587) originally was of Trajan in bronze. I tried to walk around the column and make out the figures on the lowest drum. I did, but it made no sense to me. Amy said, "And you pride yourself on being a Historian. Ha!" I said, "At least I like the pictures!" Checkmate.

Trajan's Column, Rome

It was all very exciting for Gaherty the sometime student of history, but in the Americas, Portugal and Spain. Back to your roots, the Romans would say. I wondered if the Romans offered ladders to curious readers. And insurance.

Then came the Trevi Fountain (no water, mon, "em obras" [under construction]), all that morning. That did not stop the tourists from bouncing coins onto the stone bottom of the Fountain. I could only recall big busted Anita Eckberg lazing about in the fountain in better days in the movie "La Dolce Vita." When I mentioned it to Amy she just said, "Figures, huh! Did they float?"

The Trevi Fountain, Rome

Time for lunch at a Trattoria on the Via Veneto. We loaded up on the local pasta and spaghetti sauce, a green salad and just one glass of wine. We were supposed to be with a Princess guide for a huge day tomorrow, so made the best of it that long Rome p.m. with a list the reader won't believe. Someone said later, "Mike and Amy, give it a rest. Only 20 days to go."

THE PANTHEON ("EM OBRAS")

The Pantheon. This is the best-preserved building of ancient Rome; it was covered with scaffolding when we were there. It was built by Emperor Agrippa in 27A.D. for worship of pagan divinities and was reconstructed by Hadrian in 80 A.D. In 609 A.D. Pope Boniface IV with permission of the emperor Phocas made it a Christian church: St. Mary of the Martyrs, and many of the bodies of those in the catacombs were moved here. The portico was of bronze, removed by Pope Urban VIII (1623 - 1644) and used by Bernini for the high altar of St. Peter's. We learned such "borrowings" were standard procedure, new church, old church. The Pantheon had statues of Agrippa and Caesar Augustus. The height and diameter of the interior are the same: 142 feet; there is a thirty-foot hole in the top center for air and light: for prayer to ascend to the sky. (Amy, "What about rain?" I said, "The Christian slaves were issued mops.") There are seven niches for pagan divinities and in the center a statue of Jove Ultor who supposedly punished Caesar's assassins. Currently the Pantheon has tombs of artists and kings, including those of Rafael and Victor Emmanuel II. It is considered the Italian national church. There! That proves the borrowings were worth the effort!

The Pantheon, Exterior, Rome

When we saw the original script above the pillars (loosely translated by a non- Latin speaker, "Agrippa did it."), I couldn't help but remember Mel Brooks' "History of the World, Part I," Rome when the comedian Comicus with soon to be freed slave joker buddy saw an inscription, something like, "Helenus sic tempus fugit." Comicus, in character, said, "I didn't know Helen was sick, but I guess it wasn't for long."

And the interior, would you go to church here? Masses are long, liturgy is emphasized. No seats or chairs, but, uh, lots of standing room.

The Pantheon, Interior, Rome

Photo Attributed: By Macrons – Own Work – CC BY – S.A. 4.0, https//com

In the vicinity, we made a very quick visit to the headquarters church of the Jesuits, Il Gesú. The reader may remember my years of education with said religious order and my constant reminders to readers in sundry books, whether apropos or not, that the Order was ordered (ha ha) out of all Spanish and Portuguese possessions in 1767 by Portugal's Marqués de Pombal for, uh, possessing too much. Their missions ("Reducciones") in southern Brazil and especially Paraguay were immensely successful, innovative, and profitable. Why booted out? They were protecting the Guarani Indians from greedy and bloodthirsty slave and gold hunters. And, uh, it is possible other religious orders were jealous. This is not official history, but my own speculation. Hollywood got it right with Robert de Niro and Jeremy Irons in "The Mission." This is for the record first mention in this book.

My lousy photo shows the Façade of Il Gesu: the Church of the Jesuits and founder Ignacio Loyola; he worked and lived at its side. I took the photo out. We had seen his early digs in Aspeitia in Basque Spain, the original Loyola castle. It took a spent cannonball in the leg to get him to forget battle, glory, riches and women. On the other hand, we do have the Spiritual Exercises and high schools, colleges and universities throughout the world. Perhaps the reader (you know, that one) may remember the Jesuit Father from AT's Portugal – Spain trip and how he and a certain Italian countess's paths crossed.

Back to the lousy picture, our Michelin guide book said the façade was an outstanding example of the Baroque architecture of the times. Okay. What seemed Baroque (and I studied Baroque Spanish literature but not architecture) was the interior. We walked up the main isle, looked up, got a bit dizzy and vamoosed. We would however compare it to other visitations – like to the Vatican and to Santa Maria Maggiore to come.

Il Gesu, Interior, Rome

PIAZZA VENEZIA AND MONUMENT TO VITTORIO EMMANUEL II

Time was moving on and so was sunlight. Piazza Venezia at dusk: it highlights one entire side of the huge monument to Victor Emmanuel II from 1885. There are volumes written about this structure. I'll try to keep it simple. The style intentionally imitates the classic architecture of Greece and Rome (the aim was to outdo both). The "monument of national unity" is giving honor to the man who succeeded in unifying Italy! (Some say it didn't work.) Don't get into a discussion about this on the street with an Italian ("We Italians can't agree on anything"), but on the other hand, you might insult him if you denied its success.

Victor Emmanuel II Monument, Rome

What I remember is that we made the mistake of sitting down at a tiny table at this terrific bar overlooking the huge square and all the traffic. The result in 1989 was the $6.50 beer (9000 lire) in a "proper"

Italian small glass! It was just one of many of our first "lessons" on getting to know Italy. I was in a state of shock at both the price and the size of the glass. Folks back home would use it for the "shooter." (I discovered prices in bars escalate if one sits down, the table fee.) Amy was shocked as well, as one can see; I think she was just tired. But the terrific time spent watching traffic in Rome at perhaps its busiest square and the melee of disorganization was entirely worth it! I have never nursed a small glass of beer like that, ever! Waiters hovered or lurked about us waiting for us to vacate the table. I told Amy, "They look like vultures in formal attire." Why did we linger? A traffic policeman in a white uniform and white pith helmet grew exhausted blowing the whistle amongst the pandemonium of Rome's drivers. Nothing historic here but one of great memories of Rome. I did chide Amy a bit about the hairdo; she said she wanted to blend in with Princess's lady passengers.

Amy, the Bar and Beer

After that exhausting afternoon we returned to the Via Veneto near the hotel and ate scallopini for an early dinner on our own! We were discovering that anything with meat in it came thinly sliced; not like the "bife" in Rio de Janeiro or Rib Eye in the U.S.! But the sauces were mouthwatering! The trattoria was a quiet respite from the street noise of Rome and then "home" to the hotel, exhausted and thinking of tomorrow's huge day, but this time in the company of a hilarious guide (Roman to be sure) hired by Princess.

DAY TWO IN ROME – THE VATICAN STATE

Catholics were not necessarily the majority of folks on this trip, and I recalled from previous "Adventurer" trips debating with those of a different persuasion, or at least discussing, the role of Rome and the Church. We ran into that again with the same Adventurer, a Mr. Owens from Cleveland. I couldn't believe he signed up again, but he said, "Let bygones be bygones, Professor." Uh, don't know if it is related, but he got his welcome to Rome. As we lined up in groups led by the Princess guide to head first to the Vatican Museum, he was swarmed by three gypsies on the Via Veneto, yelled for help and managed to free himself along with some help from yours truly. The gypsies knew the score and fled down the street. He did manage a "thank you" while muttering about the damned Italians, the damned Romans and, yeah, the damned gypsies. I quipped, "Those gypsies weren't Catholic Mr. Owens; what you needed were the Swiss Guards!" The guide, Guiseppe quipped, "It happens all the time to the tourists. The Romans just keep a 10,000 lire bill handy for bribes. Folks, hang on to your purses and wallets and documents, and hopefully you have a fancy money belt."

So, we all succeeded in walking down what seemed 100 steps to the subway entrance, Guiseppe flashed some card to the operator and soon we were whisked off to the Vatican. With a few hundred other tourists we were dropped at "the side gate" for entrance first to the Museum. I would have preferred the huge Piazza San Pietro, but, patience, it would come later. Oh, the highlight was walking by a huge bakery on the street, seeing guys dressed in white t-shirts and shorts rolling dough. The bread scent was wonderful and overwhelming.

Miss Amy was once again in "Cruise Attire" rather than AT. She said, "Get used to it until we are on board." First thing we saw was the sculpture display before we actually went inside the Museum. Guisseppe said, "It's worth millions, dollars I mean; the best of its kind in the world." Uh oh, a Roman Rotarian!

Here's the guy with the snakes; it is famous. Okay. The guide: "This is the famous Laocoon group. It was sculpted during the second half of the first century A.D., found at Nero's Golden House on the Esquiline Hill by Sangallo and Michelangelo. The mythology behind the sculpture: Laocoon, a priest of Apollo, incurred Apollo's wrath and was crushed to death, along with his two sons, by serpents." Amy and I would adopt that tourist's mantra from Trajan's Column, in private, "Who cares!" And we also were about in convulsions remembering the AT tourist's unforgettable remark when we were all in the Prado a few years ago. Seeing Velázquez's "Las Meninas," the young lady said, "I hate this shit." Amy and I would memorize and repeat the mantra many, many times over the years.

The Laocoon Group, Vatican Museum

Wonky, of fame from past AT trips, quipped, "I know a snake in the grass when I see one." He just was not ready for all this "high culture."

My own favorite in the museum which left us all dazed and confused was this beauty in stained glass,

Madonna and Child, the Vatican Museum

Quite a different view of Mary and Jesus from what we knew. Astounding in its beauty! One of the more informed "Adventurers" piped up, "She's a spittin' image of one of the Médici daughters. I bet some strings were pulled by a friendly Pope to get this done. Jesus, well, is confident with his covering." Guffaws from nearby. Seriously, the image is gorgeous! His wife said, "I'd kill for that robe!" So perhaps 1500 years after Jesus, in Rome, this was the perhaps inevitable view. Someone said, "That isn't Mary and Jesus." Who knows?

But then we were escorted to the nearby, connecting Sistine Chapel. All joking stopped and we marveled at the overwhelming scenes in front, to the side and above us.[2] No photos, but I managed to obtain a facsimile of one of Michelangelo's highlights:

Reproduction, the Last Judgement, the Sistine Chapel

Sorry, I didn't get the most famous, "The Creation," but "The Last Judgement" will have to do. There are lots of jokes about Michelangelo on his back high up on the scaffolding. One I told later, on board, if space permits or not is:

"There's this fellow way high up on a scaffold in the Sistine Chapel and he's getting a bit tired and bored. Seeing a little

---

[2] See the Sistine Chapel in all its glory in the recent movie "The Two Popes."

old Italian lady kneeling down below with a rosary in her hand, he thinks, "I'm a gonna have a little fun." So he yells out from above, "Hey, lady, this is a' Jesus." No response. He yells again, louder, "Hey lady this is a' Jesus." A tiny face looks up, she rattles her rosary beads and say, "Shuddup a sonny! I'm a talkin' to your Momma."

Seriously, most of us oohed and aahed thinking in this long room the Cardinals make their choices of the next Pope! It takes a book, and a big one, to explain it all.

After exiting and a long, long walk around what was St. Peter's on the other side, the guide said we had to see the whole shebang in proper order, so we entered. First his spiel:

THE PIAZZA SAN PIETRO AND THE CUPULA

"History: St. Peter was martyred in Rome in 64 A.D., St. Paul in 67 A.D. They had met in Jerusalem in 39 A.D. and at that time had split their mission, St. Paul to the gentiles, St. Peter to the Jews. In Rome the Christians were "blamed" for the fire in Rome during Nero's reign. Where St. Peter's Basilica is today there originally was a church built on the site of St. Peter's grave, from 320-350 A.D. Before that the site was a burial ground near Nero's and Caligula's Circuses.

"The modern St. Peter's was started in the mid - 15th century; the dome was finished in 1600 and the façade in 1612 by Bernini. Bernini added the colonnade in 1657-1667.

"The fountain on the left as you view the Basilica is by Bernini. The one on the right was by Carlo Maderno in 1612. The Obelisk is Egyptian from the 19th century B.C. and was dedicated to the Sun God. It was brought by Caligula to Rome and placed in his circus where the Vatican is now. It was moved to its current location in the center of the square in 1586.

The Bernini Fountain, Piazza San Pietro

Amy and I were not sure why the Popes allowed a pagan sun god obelisk to hang around. There's got to be more to the story. One notices a large church in the rear.

The Obelisk, St. Peter's

Then come more photos. I'm already seeing we will (pardon the farm expression) have to cull out a few hundred. You can't not give St. Peter his due:

St. Peter in Front of St. Peter's

While in that Piazza Amy and I were with Royal Princess passengers from Arkansas.

A Delightful Arkansas Connection at St. Peter's

Honestly, inside the huge St. Peter's I must have taken thirty pictures. The ones of the main altar, the Baldachin, the stained glass "Holy Spirit," and many others don't do it justice, but one "minor" site and the crowd favorite was the holy water fountain with a happy Amy to the side. The smudges on the Bernini baroque angel are not due to "messy eating" as one person quipped, but to grubby tourist hands, thousands of them, touching or rubbing this guy. We dutifully did dip fingers, some standing on tiptoe, for the blessing.

Amy, Bernini's Holy Water Font

Oh, Mr. Owens again. He did earlier amble up to us near the Baldachin bronze canopy in St. Peter's and quipped, "St. Paul's in London is better. Anglican you know. However, we still like your jokes." I quipped, "It used to be Catholic before that business of Henry VIII wanting a divorce from Spanish Queen Catherine of Aragon. Check your history, Mr. Owens."

The highlight that morning could have been the Piazza, the interior of St. Peter's, or perhaps the high view. One climbs a narrow, claustrophobic interior stairway that actually goes via the interior of the top of the huge dome, exits to a breathtaking view from the Piazza of St. Peter's.

Overview, Piazza San Pietro

One can walk around the entire top of what is called the "colonnade." I do not know who and what Bernini and others took years to create, but perhaps the apostles in the foreground and a few dozen "persons of interest" (I don't mean criminals but just important dignitaries) in the circle complete the scene. The main entrance which we did after the church is the Via della Conciliazione with the Tiber River beyond.

How we managed to do it I can't say, but Amy and I separated from the group to do two "biggies" that day.

The first was SAN PIETRO IN VINCOLI

This church is originally from the 5th century A.D. and was later restored by the Della Rovere family (Pope Julius II). It has the chains which supposedly bound Peter in Jerusalem and then Rome. Perhaps. More important to us was the famous sculpture - Michelangelo's Moses. Here's the story.

Pope Julius II wanted to build his own tomb and wanted Michelangelo to do it; he imagined a three-story marble structure for the center of St. Peter's. Michaelangelo was purportedly eight months in Carrara choosing the marble. He had fantasized of one huge statue of the whole mess. Unfortunately, Pope Julius II switched allegiance to the architect Bramante, so Michaelangelo went home to Florence a bit dejected. Good things come to he who waits! Julius died in 1513 and his successor Paul III recalled Michelangelo to restart the project. He did the Moses and was going to do another, but was then called by the Pope to finish "The Last Judgement" in the Sistine Chapel instead. Again, one must pardon tourist enthusiasm for Moses' grime (Mr. Owens said, "Doesn't the Vatican have enough dough to hire a few housekeepers? Or maybe those nuns. He needs a bath.") My take: Bernini is a master and nothing surpasses his magnificent works.

Bernini's Moses

We then dragged our bodies to the last of the biggies we wanted to see, St. Mary Major or SANTA MARIA MAGGIORE. This is one of the four major churches in Rome (St. John Lateran, San Paolo Fuori Muri, and St. Peter's are the others). We thought, two out of four ain't bad! It was started in 432 A.D. by Pope Sixtus in honor of the Virgin Mary one year after the Church Council of Ephesus in which Nestorius, Patriarch of Constantinople, claimed Mary was not the mother of God. Uh oh. So, Rome built this in response and opposition.

The reliquary is touted to contain wood from the crib of Jesus in Bethlehem!

The Reliquary. Santa Maria Maggiore

A hard act to follow, but there was a spectacular ending: this is a view of the ceiling of the church and the Baldachin. It used the first gold to come from the Americas, given to Pope Alexander VI (1492-1503). Perhaps this is explained by the fact he was both a Spaniard and a Borgia. The gift came from the Catholic Kings Fernando and Isabella.

The Baldechin Ceiling, Santa Maria Maggiore

Exhausted and overwhelmed, we got the subway back to the Via Veneto and to a great dinner, the full works, at Tullio's Trattoria, a Rome experience. The wine flowed as did the conversation. We were joined by the Peixotos from Brazil, did much reminiscing of past AT trips, and each one of us got a chance to opine on highlights thus far. For my new reader, Senhor Peixoto is a retired diplomat from Brazil, knew Vinicius de Morais and drank real scotch with him ("not the Brazilian stuff"), and is accompanied by his very cool Carioca wife Uiara. We have clicked on two past AT trips. They both knew Rome well, but wanted the Royal Princess "Dez Cantos" business. We shall see them often.

THE NEXT AND LAST DAY – ANCIENT ROME

Amy and I were both were looking forward to it, but would agree when it was over, enough already! Not to say we did not appreciate it, but ruins are ruins. Lots of rocks, columns, and perhaps incredible pieces of history awaited us. Oh, a note to the curious reader: neither of us were "on duty" until boarding the Royal Princess and that would be in Venice. Right now, we were still "regular" Adventurers. After a caffé con latte off we went on the subway to the Colosseum. Here's my blurb on the Colosseum and its history:

In 72 AD Vespasian, a Flavian emperor, wanted a place for public entertainment, so he used the space previously occupied by Nero's lake and built the largest Roman amphitheater in the world. There was a huge statue of Nero found nearby, 120 feet high, his head surrounded by rays of the sun. Modesty was evidently not his forté. Seats were allotted according to social station; women sat at the top under a colonnade; slaves stood on the terraces. Gladiators marched in in rank, dressed in purple and gold, right arms raised, saying: "Ave, Imperator, Morituri te salutant". "Hail, Emperor, from those who salute you and are about to die."[3]

There was an underground warren for animals which would be killed in the arena or would kill unarmed Christians. The coliseum was inaugurated in 80 A.D. by Emperor Titus with one hundred days of spectacles: races, duels between gladiators, and men and wild animals. Later, naval engagements were held in a flooded arena. In 249 A.D., the millennium of the founding of Rome, there was a huge bloodletting.

In the 16th century the coliseum became a quarry for the city of Rome; its stones were used to build the Piazza Venezia (in front of Victor Emmanuel II) and St. Peter's. It was consecrated at this time to the memory of the Christian martyrs (the cross in the photo).

---

[3] Once again, my mind is filled with cinema: Russell Crow in "The Gladiator" and Joaquin Phoenix an evil Roman emperor.

Exterior, the Colosseum

Mike, Interior of the Colosseum

What may have been a highlight was what we saw out front! A beautiful blushing bride with her new husband, a Bently providing transportation, and the scene a nice souvenir of the wedding day. Amy said, "Okay, country boy, do this for me and I'll dig up that engagement ring and we'll have a go at it!" They had to be nobility or descendants of old Vic Emmanuel. Funny, huh? The tourists behind did not take notice. Just another wedding in front of the Colosseum.

Bride and Groom, the Colosseum

An unexpected thrill was to see one of Rome's trolley lines; it matched the cars we rode in Lisbon years earlier.

Electric Trolley, Rome

THE ARCH OF CONSTANTINE

If you can't top the Colosseum, you can at least build something next door! The purpose of arches under the Romans is still debated, but each was probably constructed to commemorate a great feat by a general - emperor, generally a war or a campaign in the Empire. But arches were used later by many nations including France in Paris, Madrid in Spain, etc. There were several more in the Roman Forum up the street; one will suffice. I can't keep them all straight yet, but each Emperor did his own. This one had a big claim to fame, just a few details (I can't include the dozen photos I took):

Constantine's Arch. One scene depicts two incidents in the wars of Emperor Marcus Aurelius. There are two medallions which represent: a) the hunt b) a sacrifice to Silvanus, God of the forest. Another side had Marcus Aurelius addressing his army; a second: a sacrificial ceremony. The Medallions: first - bear hunting, second: a sacrifice to Diana, goddess of the hunt and huntress.

Constantine's Arch, Rome

Up the street on the left will be the maze of buildings of the Imperial Forum [Il Fiori Imperioli], but this is a good shot of that huge thoroughfare we saw before. The "Via Dei Fiori Imperioli."

Via dei Fiori Imperioli

43

THE ROMAN FORUM

This was the true center of ancient Rome; the imperial forum is across the street from today's thoroughfare, the Via dei Fiori Romani, and was built in honor of the diverse emperors, Julius Caesar on. But the Roman Republic was established about 500 years before that. Rome had defeated Greece in approximately 400 B.C. One shot shall suffice. I can't begin to include the two dozen more photos of arches, columns, remains of buildings, statues, all important in the Michelin Guide.

The Roman Forum

On we go, the last place chosen on this outing. The following photo is the stairway up to the Capitoline (Piazza del Campidoglio). The two statues with two knights standing beside their horses (presumably Castor and Pollux) are from the late empire; they were found in the 16th C. on the Campus Martius and moved here. Pope Paul III in 1536 decided that the hill should be restored to its former elegance in honor of the visit of Carlos V Emperor of Spain and the Holy Roman Empire, an Austrian, in 1536.

Ha! Carlos V had sacked Rome in 1527! Michelangelo was contracted to draw up the plans for the Capitolium. It took 100 years to finish.

Piazza dei Campidoglio

There was a sculpture I can't leave out: one source says it is the River God Tiberius (hence the Tiber River) with the cornucopia. I'm sure they hauled it in from somewhere else. I'll bet Bernini has his name on it. But can't say, just can't say.

The River God Tiberius

Okay, that did it for old Rome. We concluded the walk had taken years off our lives. Would be do it again? Of course. That night we did room service in the hotel. Whew.

LAST MORNING IN ROME

The last morning, Amy and I took off on our own, an early morning getaway; later there would be a rush to the hotel for the super-duper train to Venice. In a way it was all backwards; we should have seen what follows before we went to St. Peter's, but the guide's plan (I think based on Rome's traffic) had started with the Vatican Museum on the other side of this scene. This was our first time to see what follows. We would have missed it otherwise due to time constraints and Princess's plan.

THE SANT'ANGELO BRIDGE AND CASTEL' SANT'ANGELO - HISTORY

The bridge across the famous Tiber was originally built by the Roman Emperor Hadrian in 136 A.D. linking the "Campus Martius" to the original site of his mausoleum. It was rebuilt in 17th century and ten baroque angels were added by Bernini.

Sant' Angelo Bridge, Rome

The Castel' on the other side of the river connected to the Vatican intended as Hadrian's sepulcher was constructed with a square base and a drum shape on top. Originally Hadrian's statue and a chariot were on the top. It has a lot of history, then and after. In 270 A.D. the Castel' became a fortress built by Emperor Aurelian.

In 590 A.D. Pope Gregory reigned; supposedly the plague ceased when the Pope saw an "angel" on top of the Castel.

The "Passeto" is a wall and corridor from the Castel to the Vatican. In 1527 the Castel became a refuge for Pope Clement VII from troops of Holy

Roman Emperor Carlos V of Spain-Austria. The pope was held prisoner and the Sistine Chapel was used as a stable by Carlos V's troops. We can't figure this one out! Why? The Holy Roman Emperor, the King of Catholic Spain and the devastation he did in Rome? Got to read up on this. Perhaps a rare reader will do the same. As a publisher in Brazil told me, "You've got to stop somewhere."

In 1870 Italy was united and the Castel became a barracks, today a museum.

We both could do no less than remember Hollywood, Tom Hanks and "Angels and Demons" for scenes in the Castel and the Piazza Navone which follows.

Castel' Sant' Angelo, Rome

THE "PIAZZA NAVONA"

In 86 A.D. it was Domitian's stadium for games in the Greek style and of the Odeon. It was stripped in 356 by Emperor Constantine. The lanes and streets are from the papal era of Renaissance Rome. In 1471 – 1484 it was the commercial center of the city. In the 16th century it became the residential area for cardinals, ambassadors, papal officials, rich bankers, and illuminators of manuscripts. This is the plaza that has the Fontana dei Fiumi – The Fountain of the 4 Rivers by Bernini done for Pope Innocent X in 1651. We both agreed what a way to finish tourism in Rome! And there was the underwater scene from "Angels and Demons" with Tom Hanks getting wet.

Fontana dei Fiumi, Roma

CANTO II

VENICE

After that last terrific scene in the Piazza Navona, there then was a hurried walk back to our hotel, pack the bags and on to Princess's treat – the electric train to Venice and new adventure. Hmm, 40 pages to do Rome and now it's only the start of Canto II. I doubt most will go over five! Uh, except perhaps Istanbul and Athens.

Princess took us by bus from the Ambasciatore to the big Termini for all the trains departing Rome. It was the electric high speed, luxury train to Venice. We shared a comfortable compartment with the Peixotos from Brazil, talking just one of the many times on the trip, this time of Rome. The huge lunch featured linen tablecloth with napkins, flowers on the table, dining with spumante and "aperitivos" of salami and bacon rolls, then the pasta course, penne a la bella donna, then the main course of vitello u broccoli, then chocolate cake and espresso, vino rosé. We could have used a nap, but it was too exciting to see the Italian countryside roll by. And that was just for openers!

ARRIVAL IN VENICE

(Mike the Historian had to borrow from tourist guides like Michelin to do this intro. Every book has anachronisms. This is mine. It saved the day.) If one is serious about all this, the following paragraphs fill the bill.

"The city was historically the capital of the Republic of Venice for almost a millennium, from 810 to 1797. It was a major financial and maritime power during the Middle Ages and Renaissance, and a staging area for the Crusades and the Battle of Lepanto against the Turks (in which, by the way, Miguel de Cervantes, lost the use of one arm, hence "El Manco de Lepanto"), as well as an important center of commerce—especially silk, grain, spice, and of art from the 13th century to the end of the 17th. The city-state of Venice is considered to have been the first real international financial center, emerging in the 9th century and reaching its greatest prominence in the 14th century. This made Venice a wealthy city throughout most of its history. For centuries Venice possessed numerous territories along the Adriatic Sea and within the Italian peninsula, leaving a significant impact on the architecture and culture that can still be seen today. The Venetian Arsenal is considered by several historians to be the first factory in history, and was the base of Venice's naval power. The sovereignty of Venice came to an end in 1797, at the hands of Napoleon. Subsequently, in 1866, the city became part of the Kingdom of Italy.

"In building its maritime commercial empire, Venice dominated the trade in salt, acquired control of most of the islands in the Aegean, including Crete and Cyprus in the Mediterranean, and became a major power-broker in the Near East. By the standards of the time, Venice's stewardship of its mainland territories was relatively enlightened and the citizens of such towns as Bergamo Brescia, and Verona rallied to the defense of Venetian sovereignty when it was threatened by invaders.

"Venice remained closely associated with Constantinople, being twice granted trading privileges in the Eastern Roman Empire, through the so-called golden bulls or "chrysobulls", in return for aiding the Eastern Empire to resist Norman and Turkish incursions. In the first chrysobull, Venice acknowledged its homage to the empire; but not in the second, reflecting the decline of Byzantium and the rise of Venice's power.

"Venice became an imperial power following the Fourth Crusade, which, having veered off course, culminated in 1204 by capturing and sacking Constantinople and establishing the Latin Empire. As a result of this conquest, considerable Byzantine plunder was brought back to Venice. This plunder included the gilt bronze horses from the Hippodrome of Constantinople which were originally placed above the entrance to the cathedral of Venice, St. Mark's Basilica (The originals have been replaced with replicas, and are now stored within the basilica.) After the fall of Constantinople, the former Eastern Roman Empire was partitioned among the Latin crusaders and the Venetians. Venice subsequently carved out a sphere of influence in the Mediterranean known as the Duchy of the Archipelago, and captured Crete.

"The seizure of Constantinople proved as decisive a factor in ending the Byzantine Empire as the loss of the Anatolian themes, after Manzikert. Although the Byzantines recovered control of the ravaged city a half-century later, the Byzantine Empire was terminally weakened, and existed as a ghost of its old self, until Sultan Mehmet the Ottoman Turk Conqueror took the city in 1453.

Not bad for openers, huh? You can see, it's a good intro to what we would see the next few days! My account of our time in Venice now follows.

The train slowed as we neared Venice and its canals. It actually BACKED into the station or stop not twenty yards from the water! We and our baggage were transferred to a vaporetto and after about twenty rapid minutes in the water, made a turn, and there in front of us in all its glory was the ROYAL PRINCESS! I note once again the passenger capacity of 800; 100 were "Adventurers" from AT. We were introduced to a very busy captain, purser and on shore coordinator (more later) on them, and scheduled a meeting to talk of joint duties and responsibilities.

Mike, Amy, the Royal Princess

After settling into our very comfortable cabin which would be home away from home for almost three weeks, we had snacks in one of many "bistros." While most Adventurers and others were settling in and getting to know the ship, or I suspect heading to its bars or small casino, Amy and I made one of the best decisions of what would come!

Princess had a vaporetto available (for Princess travelers only) to go on into the center of Venezia. We chose that ride (the only takers that late afternoon) for a private introduction to Venice! It turned out to be an early highlight of the trip.

The first astounding view of the Piazza San Marco in Venice! "La Libreria de San Marco" to the left; the "Palacio Ducale" to the right! (I use Spanish when in doubt.)

Piazza San Marco, Venice

As I said, we were the only ones on the vaporetto! We had about twenty minutes alone to take in that magnificent introductory view of Venice as we drew up to the "servizio gondole" and docks. No history yet! We spent almost two hours in the main piazza which was filled in early evening with dining tables, and no less than three separate small orchestras were entertaining the crowds. We immediately recognized, what else, VIVALDI! It was incredibly romantic and a wonderful start to this wonderful place. (I have not said yet, the famous lady orchestra conductor who was with us in AT's Portugal and Spain trip was along. There would be many long conversations at sea talking of the classical music of the era.) Amy and I nursed glasses of wine while listening to what seemed like violin "virtuosi." Entertainment was also one slightly tipsy gentleman who stood up and conducted the music perfectly from his table! We then strolled along the canal watching the gondolas come and go and heard continuous singing. We arrived to where Princess's vaporetto had left us off, boarded and once again, enjoyed the jaunt to the ship in what seemed like a dream trip just for the two of us. We agreed later we would never have traded this experience for anything! The Romantic personified! I could have proposed again, but, uh, I didn't.

There was one "downer;" back aboard ship my famous (for the professor) touchy stomach acted up and I had my first bout ending with Pepto Bismol. A hot shower and bedtime ruled. Tomorrow would be the main and only day to see Venice.

THE NEXT DAY IN VENICE

Along with the crowds (normal they say) we this time in the a.m. were free to see whatever we could in the morning and return to the ship for a big lunch. There was a guide available whose English was suspect, but we were able to sidle away. Princess would depart late that afternoon for the high seas. I can't begin to include here all the photos we took, but offer a few to peruse. I'll comment on just a few of them. A note: the weather was perfect and Venice was not experiencing the famous "high tides" of winter that are known to flood all the piazzas and streets.

Now, with the crowds and, ahem, came the other crowds of pigeons which, pardon a maritime term, "inundate" the streets and tourists' heads and shoulders with, well, pigeon poop. Some say the pigeons of San Marcos are romantic and Venice would not be the same without them. Not me. Princess's guide said earlier, "Wear hats." Wonky, our ever-entertaining veteran of many Adventurer trips, ever Wonky, said, "Pardon me, it's not raining today, is the sun that strong?" The answer would come soon enough.

My photos of the Piazza don't do it justice; it is just too immense to capture with all the crowds of people. For what it's worth, I can offer blurbs of what we saw:

Most impressive is "Il Palazzo Ducale" with the statue of San Teodoro to the left on the column. The bronze lion from the right one is gone. One of the Adventurers, a Brit known for his photography and love of nature, made a pithy remark, "Well, we weren't promised animals, birds and nature on this trip. I see why. A good thing. Somebody nipped the lion." (Laughter by us who knew him.)

Piazza San Marco, Entrance

To the left of the Palazzo is the famous "Torre del Orologio." The Watch Tower built from 1496 to 1499. The bell is rung on the hour by the dark bronze figures called "Moros". (Hmm, we know about them.) Below the bell, the Virgin stands (the doors open and figures of an angel and the magi pass in front of her on the feast of the Ascension). Our adventurer said in a loud voice to anyone who would listen, "Oops, my fault; they just moved the lion." It turns out they are everywhere, after all, the symbol of

St. Mark and Venice. And lots of horses if you kept your eyes open, but way high up.

Il Torre del Orologio

The front of "San Marco:" note the gold lion way up and the four bronze horses amidst the scaffolding. Mike safely ensconced in his white Portuguese fisherman's hat is amongst the crowd.

The Façade of San Marco

It was then we saw our first wonderful mosaics of Venice (but far from the last, including others in Istanbul). The front of the Palazzo San Marco: mosaics of the Resurrection and the Ascension.

Mosaic at the Entrance, San Marco

Inside the Palazzo, this one of the Virgin rivaled or surpassed those on the outside.

Mosaic of the Virgin, Interior, San Marco

I think she is accompanied by the Evangelist John on her right and home town hero St. Mark on her left.

It is, after all, the "Doge's Palazzo" so it was difficult to choose one of many famous paintings of the fellow or fellows (there were many of them over time), "Doge" meaning "Duque" and ruler and main man. I chose this one, the Doge Pietro Loredan implores the Virgin to end the famine. (J. Tintoretto).

The Doge Implores the Virgin

Il Collegio" (the Council Chamber) Or Another Room, My Possible Error

The guide book says the paintings in the ceiling were commissioned from Veronese, who completed them between 1575 and 1578. "This ceiling is one of the artist's masterpieces and celebrates the Good Government of the Republic, together with the Faith on which it rests and the Virtues that guide and strengthen it." (Michelin) Other paintings are by Tintoretto and show various Doges with Christ, the Virgin and saints.

The Ceiling of the Council Chamber

Amy looked at me and whispered, "I hate this shit." However, we had worked up an appetite and chose the option of returning to the ship for what the Chef called "a light lunch." Ha! More later. Oh, I forgot, somewhere in the maze of buildings connected to the Palazzo was a famous but small bridge, "The Bridge of Sighs." "Ponti dei sospiri." The English name from Lord Byron. It connected interrogation rooms in the Doge' Palace with, gulp, the prison, but provided prisoners' last view of Venice!

The rest of the afternoon (but warned to be back by 4:00 p.m.) we were allowed to be on our own. My reader (s) already know Amy and I can "make tracks" when necessary to see the sites. Uh oh. A chance to plug the entire series of Adventurer books in Brazil, Mexico, Portugal and Spain, Guatemala, Colombia and now The Mediterranean. We hopped a vaporetto in the main canal, saw several famous bridges (Il Rialto, Ponte della Accademia) before getting off at the Ca'Doro [Golden Dock]. We walked along very narrow sidewalks aside small waterways or "rivas" and saw a lot of what the locals saw in Venice – fruit stands and markets, a

Muraro glass factory (the glass chandeliers of Venice decorate much of Europe), and a plaza with the famous statue of Colleoni, the "Condottiere" of Venice from 1481- 1490, the military captain who ran things. A bit like "El Cid" in Spain. A clerk in a nearby shop shared a local joke with us. "He was called by some 'Tre Colliere' a play on words meaning, I apologize, three testicles, thus explaining his extraordinary feats." Amy had to say, "Three must be better than two."

But our final memory of Venice could not have been better. On the walk back to the ship passing just one of the many canals, we witnessed a real donnybrook of a scene between one of the famous Gondolier oarsmen and tourists. Evidently the latter did not catch either his Italian or fractured "tourist English" and understood 10,000 lire instead of 100,000! We left when he was talking very loudly to a fellow gondolier oarsman down the way, saying, "Who the #$%^& do these @#$%^^ tourists think they are?" The photo captures it all; I think he is explaining (counting) lire for them. He later in very rapid Italian explained to a colleague coming down the canal the cause of his frustration and anger.

The Gondolier Counts Money

Time was moving on and we really had to walk fast through narrow side streets, dead end streets and others before finding our way back to the quay and catch the vaporetto to the Royal Princess. Sorry, we never took the gondola ride!

But somebody really planned our departure from Venice – a very slow glide of Princess out of the lagoon but passing the Piazza San Marco and all we had seen. Tonight would be the first luxurious dinner on board, in our case we were invited to the Captain's private dining room. After all, we would be liaison between AT and RP crew and staff.

Amy and I were introduced to several of the RP staff, some we would be working with: Captain Timothy (Tim) Johannsen, purser Jennifer (Jenni) Donaldson, on shore excursions coordinator Sally Reynolds, and techie Joseph (Joe) Spivey who handled microphones in the speaker's podium in the huge lounge with windows in all directions. We had dinner with them in the small, private dining room of crew, one deck below the bridge. Captain's quarters and others were just down the way.

The quick "cook's tour" that followed was a bit scary (because it was night) - pitch black reflections on the waves from the ship's lights, this on the promenade deck. "Amy, you're not on AT' 'International Traveler' in Cambodia anymore," I quipped to Amy. We saw the small casino, the movie theater, and the larger show room where the live entertainment would come. Sleep, that's what we wanted.

CANTO III

DUBROVNIK

The next morning, 9 a.m. and it was Mike to work! This was my first cultural introduction on board, honestly not Noble Prize Worthy, but the microphone worked well as I stood on the observation deck and recited my lines as we pulled into a spectacular view of this important medieval city. Was I nervous this first time around on RP? Do I need to mention it? Sally Reynolds would say later, "Not bad, just okay. You get a pass for the first one but I'm expecting more at Crete, Heraklion and Knossos!" I was put on the spot.

"Dubrovnik is the main tourist site on the Adriatic Sea today; it started as a Greek trading post, then the Romans conquered the area, later, Slavonic tribes conquered and pillaged the Roman town of Epidaurus or Cavtat. The area really came into its own during medieval times as Ragusa which found itself under Byzantine, Venetian and the Croation - Hungarian Kingdom at different times. The Independent Republic of Ragusa rivaled Venice in commerce. The name is from the Greek "argosy," "merchant treasure ship." Dubrovnik is located on the south Dalmatian coast, the southernmost part of Croatia. Ragusa after its heyday fell to the Ottoman Empire in the 14th century.

Later history:
1806: Napoleon occupies Dubrovnik for nine years.

1814: Dubrovnik is given to the Austrian Empire.

1914: Archduke Ferdinand, heir to the Austrian Hapsburg throne, is assassinated in Saravejo; WW I begins.

1917: Dubrovnik is now in the Republic called Yugoslavia.

1941: Hitler invades and occupies.

1943: Marshall Tito of the Yugoslav Communist partisans throws out the Germans and rules until 1980.

For the reader: all was calm in 1989, but we were told Croatians, Serbians and Yugoslavs were feeling "edgy" even now.

Princess had traveled from Venice last night and we were headed up the Dalmatia Coast early that morning and were greeted with this spectacular view of Dubrovnik.

Dubrovnik, the Harbor

We would have only the morning to get around and Amy and I got into mountain goat mode after the short formal tour by the **RP** guide (to be seen, coming up). Maybe not big news to everyone is that this is the location of the famous church of St. Blaise, he of folkloric fame as the healer of sore throats. Really. The city wall entrance features his carved image. Not folklore is the fact St. Blaise was the patron saint of Dubrovnik and Protector of the Independent Republic of Ragusa. He greets all travelers at the walled entrance to the city.

The Castle, St. Blaise, Dubrovnik

We followed the guide's tour to some places famous but not that important to us, the reason to follow, including the interior of St. Blaise's church. Amy wondered if they sold cough drops at the entrance. Ha ha. After Rome, the inside was nice, even beautiful, but just a curiosity Oh, I forgot. Did the reader notice we did not visit ANY churches in Venice? I joke now, recalling "Saturday Night Live's "Church Lady." "Isn't that special?" I was criticized more than once on the trip for not taking things so seriously. Guilty. I quipped in response to that complaint, "Oh, do you mean all the rocks?" As the reader will see, we saw lots of them in piles waiting to be appreciated (I mean the Imperial Forum in Rome just the first such case). On the other hand, a few travelers also complained I was telling too much history in the prep talks. So, here's a rock story for them: in our AT travels in Mexico and the Yucatan, we ran across an entire big field in Uxmal just lined up with rocks in neat rows. The archeologists explained: it's the GOK PILE. Meaning, "God only knows." They were talking about the Maya constructions at Tikal, Palenque, Uxmal, Chichén - Itzá or Copán and the rocks they would have to sort out, order and use to rebuild, let's say, a stairway. Sorry: the main monument at Copán in Honduras has a huge stairway with hundreds of individual stones with glyphs on each. The entire stairway was wrecked by an earthquake and the archeologists spent years putting it back together. Ahem, probably not like the Mayas intended. For Princess's purposes, I'll let the reader know with a GOKS AHEAD warning. On the other hand, the polished marble main street of Dubrovnik deserves a look.

Marbled Main Street of Dubrovnik

While most people sat at the café, delightful to be sure, Amy and I walked the city wall and were rewarded with this astounding view. Sorry, that's their GOK pile on the hill. Amy said, "Enough already, get off it."

The City Wall, Dubrovnik

The walls formed a medieval fort, 2 kilometers or 1 and 1\4 miles around, up to 18 feet thick at spots. Today's walls are the fortifications built in the 15th and 16th centuries. There are a total of 15 towers, 5 bastions, 2 corner towers and a fortress. The tallest tower is called the Mináeta. Others are the St. Dominic's tower. I must have twenty more slides of our walk, some with beautiful ocean views, so here is just one:

The Adriatic from the City Wall, Dubrovnik

Notice the cannon placed in this niche and the thickness of the wall, but the nice view when there was no battle going on. They sunbathe on the rocks below.

After that hurried walk (AT travelers in Portugal and Spain compared it to the walk around the medieval walled city of Óbidos near Sintra, entirely apropos), there was a rush back to Princess, most people tired and sweaty if not hungry. Hmm. Eight hundred passengers, cool water in the showers even for Princess!

At lunch on board there was an argument in the main dining room, a loud affair; it involved passengers over the relative merits of Venice and Dubrovnik (passengers with relatives hailing from the respective places). It did not come down to fisticuffs but we learned people on this trip had their favorites! Someone said, "It was just like this in 1500 A.D.! Times never change!" Laughter.

We would have a day and a half at sea at a very leisurely pace before Crete, so there was time for me to bone up on that introduction, but also for us to enjoy the amenities of the ship and that old seafarers' custom: the Captain's Dinner. We were supposed to mingle with passengers and that's what we did. Then at sea and, uh, seeing the ship.

We were reminded we were not on the "International Adventurer" – these people wanted to work on their tans!

Sunbathers, the Royal Princess

I thought the view down the stairway to the rear lower deck was spectacular and a bit scary. One could see the huge wake of Princess's propellers. Oh, along with the sun tan crowd, they had a place on that back deck where one could hit golf balls into the pristine Adriatic and Mediterranean.

I have not said, but Amy and I and hundreds of others were fans of the Promenade Deck where you hoped to work off calories from the always scrumptious and plentiful meals. More later on that. But one sees the reason "not to worry" or perhaps Mad Magazine's Alfred E. Newman and "What? Me worry?" There were plenty of life boats (we had done an emergency drill shortly after embarking in Venice).

The Lifeboats, the Royal Princess

Earlier that day we had breakfast with fellow Adventurers on the Lido Deck, watched the ship pass the Ithaca Strait (amazing weather, blue sky. blue water). Sally Reynolds took over and gave a preview of grandeur to come: Izmir, Ephesus and Istanbul. I would give more details as it came up. She was a pro, understated, entertaining and informative. Dare I say, a hard act to follow. Amy said, "Ole' boy, take notes!"

In the p.m. there was "tea," meaning, yes, British afternoon tea and an abundance of Chef Reginald's pastries. Amy and I and a favorite couple from Arkansas got up to the navigation deck (much larger and yes more impressive we had to admit than the "International Adventurer," but not as friendly, I just mean more formal, more people) and had the tour.

That night came the famous "Captain's Dinner" in the huge dining room, waiters in formal livery, and a menu we would never forget: caviar, lobster bisque, Beef Wellington, and our choice, a Portuguese red wine. As the wine flowed, so did the conversation. We were by the way in "fine dining" dress, coat and tie, nice evening dress for Amy. This was our first time with Princess Travelers. Most of the time was spent discussing and comparing Princess cruises and our own AT Expeditions. John and Mary from Cincinnati had traveled the world, he a retired surgeon (!), she a clinical psychiatrist with a successful practice she told us all about (not names, but interesting cases). They were curious, yes, and a bit sniffy, about the company they were keeping. I, ever the diplomat, and Amy, ever the good will ambassador, emphasized how wonderful it was for us and AT guests to experience this "other world" of travel. When John and Mary learned more of my education, degree, teaching experience and Amy's years of on-board logistics, their attitude seemed to soften. But Mary did say, "Have you always been at Nebraska?" The reader can read between the lines. We decided, good to have such people aboard, I mean, just in case.

On the contrary, I would meet a ridiculously wealthy Nebraska farmer later on the trip and we reminisced of Big Red Football and, ahem, the cheerleaders, crops and farm equipment and their spiraling cost (he went into great detail on the huge tractors and harvesters) and yes, you guessed it, Sand Hill Cranes on the Platte. He and wife Betsy would become familiar and fun companions later on the trip. Amy and I snuck away after dinner, perhaps for the only time, to see the short "show" in the mini-auditorium (Broadway music) and then to bed.

CANTO IV
KNOSSOS (HERAKLION, CRETE)
MINOAN CIVILIZATION

Crete, Map of Ancient Greece

Before this on-board presentation I told Sally, "This time you are going to get your money's worth – enough serious history to make your head spin." Read on:

"The Minoan Civilization on the isle of Crete was during the second millennium B.C., the high point at 1700 B.C. There was a priest – king named Minos, probably after the Minos of legend. It tells of King Minos, his daughter, the labyrinth, the minotaur, Theseus of Greece and the string he unfurled to get into the labyrinth, kill the minotaur, and rescue his sweetheart. A good story, huh? It made it into all the history books. Or at least the mythology books. The Minoans probably came from Anatolia in today's western Turkey around 3000 - 1100 BC. The Palace at Knossos dates from 1700 B.C. There was a sudden disappearance of the Minoan civilization perhaps due to volcanic activity.

110 - 67 B.C. Dorian Greeks invade and classical Greece controls.

67 B.C. – A.D. 120. Romans invade, make Gortnya their capital; St.Paul is here in 59 A.D. and brings Christianity to the isle.

395 A.D. Crete becomes part of the Byzantine Empire.

A.D. 823: Saracens (Moslems) conquer Crete and they establish the town which is to become Heraklion.

961 A.D.: the Byzantines liberate Crete from the Moslems.

1204 A.D.: the 4th Crusade. Byzantium falls and Crete is sold to Venice and Venetians build the harbor and the fort at Heraklion.

16th and 17th century: This is Crete's renaissance period. El Greco (Dominikos Theotokopoulous) of Spanish painting fame and Toledo was from here and moved to an apprenticeship in Rome.

1648: Turks take the island; this becomes the Dark Ages for Heraklion.

1898: Great Britain, France, Russia and Italy expel the Turks; Crete becomes an autonomous part of the Ottoman Empire.

1913: Crete becomes part of Greece.

1941: Germans take the island and occupy it.

1944: The Allies take the island. It once again becomes part of Greece.

Miscellaneous:

The Minoans were a great naval power of the Mediterranean in their day of 1700 B.C. as well as a great commercial power. They were known for the "bull jumpers" and the "bull cult" (the antecedent of the bullfight in Spain). There are statues of bulls throughout the Mediterranean, including at Ephesus in Roman times. The frescoes and mosaics of Heraklion are famous: the Minoan woman, the dolphins, others.

What can I say? First, ahem, about this "bull jumping," we saw no evidence of it, but had to recall our AT trip to Colombia in 1982 when we witnessed real "bull jumping" in a country bullfight in Boyacá State. A "matador" – clown dressed like Superman with the red cape and carrying a vaulting pole, did exactly that – run straight ahead toward the bull and vault over it! Hmm. Had he been reading weighty tomes about Crete? We just laughed. Now, the bad news: the stop was not all that impressive. Maybe Princess needed to "gas up." Ha. The reconstruction of the ruins was, well, reconstruction. The good news: the reader (s) only needs to see just a few photos. This first, the painting of the Minoans' love of dolphins.

Painting of the Minoans' Dolphins

Does the reader now see what I mean? i.e., reconstruction. I think the history is true, but the legend and stories are better. Here's what's left of the Heraklion Palace of Minos: granted there were some old mosaics and paintings on the walls. For your information, what appears below is NOT a GOK PILE. Just miscellaneous stones.

The Heraklion Palace of Minos

I'll just try to summarize the rest of the short visit to Crete.

At some point the on – shore guide made a very big deal of the first "sewer" system: a series of canals always with moving water which carried waste away from the bathrooms. The first "john" is proudly shown to tourists. When you think about it, it is really very important. Amy and I were moved to think of Palenque in Mexico and that there a small stream was diverted through the main palace for exactly the same reason. We are talking Mayas from 300 to 900 A.D. Amy quipped, "Better than that two hole on the farm in Nebraska, huh? Were you as 'civilized' as these folks?"

Most impressive to us was the manmade sea wall allowing all the ships to dock at this place. We see the Royal Princess in all her glory; there were perhaps a dozen small cruise ships with Greek names in the same harbor.

The Princess and Sea Wall at Heraklion

Maybe that wind was part of the "front" we would experience that night at sea.

I commented (in private to Amy) that the countryside of Heraklion had lots of olive groves and vineyards but seemed unusually dry and also very barren. A query: was this due to four thousand years of sheepherding and farming?

I needed a shower and nap. Dinner that evening was prime rib and Yorkshire pudding. So far, for the only time on the trip, it was a rough evening and night, the ship rolling in fierce wind. As a Nebraska landlubber this seemed a mystery to me for a ship like Princess, but not to Amy. "Don't ever underestimate the ocean. There's a reason for shipwrecks." I said, "At least we don't have icebergs" (a reference to you know what). With two Dramamine tablets (Princess kept them in a big bowl outside the purser's office on the registration deck. I was hoping no one confused them with plain M &Ms) I did survive the experience. I forgot to mention, during that day I experienced slight vertigo, a condition

I learned was normal for persons with first days' experience at sea. They said it would pass and it did. Nebraska was never like this, except, maybe for post beer blast time after Big Red Football. I remember the Oklahoma game.

CANTO V

EPHESUS INLAND FROM IZMIR, TURKEY

The following are the notes from my introduction on board. We are seeing more and more of Greek civilization and history prior to the Romans. Only part of these comments was delivered in the lounge area on board.

Geography: Ephesus is inland from Izmir, Turkey

1000 BC: Greek colonists arrive in the area, Aeolians, then Ionians. The town of Smyrna (today Izmir) is conquered by Sardis.

334 BC. Alexander the Great (of Macedonia) and his Empire: he founded a new Smyrna and a new Ephesus.

190 BC: Rome conquers the Greeks and Ephesus becomes its capital of Asia Minor. The rise of Christianity follows with important churches at Ephesus and Smyrna. St. John's gospel was written at Ephesus.

St. Paul preached here originally; one story has it that the Virgin Mary may have spent her last days here.

Rome declines, Byzantium declines, so the Seljuk Turks enter. This is followed by the Mongolian invasion of the area. The Ottoman Turks arrive to take control in 1415.

1535: Suleiman the Great of Istanbul signs a treaty with France allowing European merchants to settle in Izmir.

19th: Ottoman Christians, Jews and Europeans settle in Izmir; the Moslems now are a minority.

20th Century. The Ottoman Turks are defeated in WWI, Britain backs a Greek invasion of Izmir, but the new Turkish Republic army under Ataturk wins from Ankara to Izmir.

1922: Fire burns the city of Izmir to the ground. A new city is started.

Miscellaneous points:

The "Agora" or market center of Alexander the Great in Izmir was rebuilt by Marcus Aurelius in 178 AD.

Sixty miles north of Izmir is the site of ancient Pergamum, as old as Troy. (Think: the "Iliad" and the "Odyssey"). It flourished during the Alexander and Hellenistic age. There was a renowned library which rivaled that of Alexandria in Egypt. When Egypt cut off its papyrus supply (for paper), Pergamum invented parchment. Alexandria's library burned to the ground later and a kind Roman Marc Antony gave Cleopatra his Pergamum collection to console her.

Ephesus was a main port and the capital of the Roman Empire in Asia Minor, but the harbor silted up in the 3rd century AD.

The pagan cult of Cybele -Artemis, an Anatolian fertility goddess, was in Ephesus before the Romans. She of the many breasts.

Our On Shore Excursion

We were not prepared for the first few hours; it seemed a continuation of dry Crete. Izmir harbor at first seemed a "poor" Rio de Janeiro along the sea, but was really depressing to us on its outskirts. There was a one and one – half hour bus ride (on a scruffy bus; AT and RP are not used to this) to Ephesus. We saw women picking cotton, two camels, a first for Mike, but I told Amy it did remind me of the covers of the Camel cigarette packages growing up, not mine, others. The area was horribly dry, dirty, trashy everywhere. We wondered, is this what all Turkey will be? One has to see the "big" picture – the amazing and important history of ancient Greece, then Rome.

Our Highlights of Ephesus.

I won't begin to show or repeat all the things we saw on the long walk on the main street through Ephesus called The Currettes Road: it went from the Heracles Gate to the Celsus Library, the center of the city; there were marble plates on the floor, covered galleries on the sides with mosaic floors; columns and the pedestals were of important personages in the city. This is a tourist site "in progress," much to be done but important, amazing places to be excavated. Uh oh. **GOK PILE WARNING.**

The Currettes' Road, Ephesus

We got a kick out of the stones (Ephesus up to this point is "king" of the **GOK PILES**) of the old baths, but mainly the names: the frigidarium, tepidarium and caldarium (cold, temperate and hot).

Next was "The Basilica." Under the Romans it was a meeting hall for debate and political or public discussion. Many people were converted into the first Christian churches after Constantine came to power, thus the name. The old Roman "stoa" in front during the Augustan period had a wooden roof with Ionic columns with bulls' heads above. Shades of Crete and the "bull jumpers."

The Noseless Bulls, Ephesus

Then came the Odeon, that is, a reconstructed "Odeon" or theater. Uh oh. The GOK pile can be seen on the other side. Seriously it took masterful study first and then hard work to rebuild important places. But sometimes it was hilarious in Ephesus, our point:

GOK Pile Put Together, Ephesus

The Odeon was used for public speaking, debate, concerts and the like and was built by an elite, small family. There were two parliaments in Ephesus's political system. The smaller which held 300 members was called the consulting parliament and it met in the Odeon.

The Odeon or Theater, Ephesus

Next was the "Dea Roma" Temple that held the "roman gods" built during and for the cult of the "deified" Emperors Augustus and son Julius Caesar. Another GOK PILE.

Next one sees the remains of the Prytaneion. The most important religious post in Ephesus was that of the Prythian responsible for the immortal fire, the hearth of the city which could never go out. It was called the "Holy Place of Hestia." We saw the Greek inscription on a column of the Prytaneion: it contains a list of the "Curettes' Union," monks from the Artemis Temple. They were in the Prytaneion to celebrate the birth of Artemis in a dramatic way. The Prytaneion was built by Augustus Caesar in the 3rd century A.D. The Greek inscription yes bears seeing:

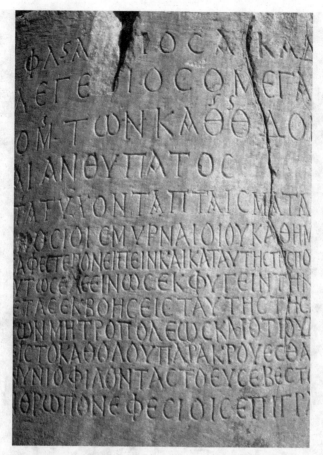

The Greek Inscription of the Times

Oh, it may be time to talk about Artemis, "She of the many breasts." She gets a full page. One can see why she got a lot of attention. And later we shall see that when St. Paul (yes that one) tried to preach in the huge amphitheater to be seen; he was interrupted by a priest of Artemis saying "Artemis is great. Artemis is better." I do not know if this is fact or legend.

Artemis in All Her Glory (ies)

I mention but do not show (GOK PILE) the Domitian Temple, an example of the "emperor's cult" in the Roman empire, not really a religion, but an institution to provide Roman unity. It was an honor for any city to be allowed to build an emperor's temple. Ephesus had four in its history:

a. Domitianus (81 - 96 A.D.) He was slain by one of his servants, rather embarrassing for a "god," so Ephesus announced his father Vespasianus to be a god and renamed the temple after him.

b. Hadrianus who came from Athens to Ephesus as Zeus Olympos.
c. Caracalla (211- 212 A.D.). He ruled jointly with his brother Geta who killed him, so he had to give up the temple in Ephesus.
d. Valerianus. 251-260 A.D.

I'm leaving out the Heracles Gate, the Nemea Lion, the remains of the Trajan Fountain and Hadrianus's Temple (it's best note is a nude Medusa, but, drat, no photo).

But then we came to the piece de resistance! The view of central Ephesus and the Celsus Library from above.

The Celsus Library

The Celsus Library, restored in 1904. It was built by the son of the Roman Pro - Consul Julius Celsus Polemeanus as a memorial and tomb for his father. On the first floor are the four statues of Virtue, Science, Fate and Wit (the originals are in Vienna; these are copies). It once had 12,000 books. Amy and I wondered if it was copied in hot west central Spain at Cáceres with its amphitheater and similar columns.

We were not done; to top it off was the Grand Theater. It faces the old harbor and was used for plays, meetings of the large public parliament, the "Demos," and had an arena for gladiators and wild animal fights in the 3rd and 4th centuries A.D. The theater had a three - floored stage. There were altars to the cult of Dionysus (Bacchus); the theater began or was born with ceremonies to Dionysus. It held 24,000 people, had plays from early morning to late night; all actors were male and they used masks to play parts.

The Grand Theater, the Demos

And finally, one sees the remains of the old road to the sea. The end of Ephesus's great importance came when the entrance silted up. The Harbor Road. It was 500 meters from the theater to the sea. It was built during the first century B.C. It was called the Arcadian Road and was used for ceremonial purposes: among them, to welcome important visitors from the sea, emperors, etc. It used to be lit; only three Roman cities had lit roads: Rome, Antioch in Syria and Ephesus.

The Harbor Road, Ephesus

Back on board after the dismal bus ride back to Izmir, showered and with drinks and reviewing our notes, we did come to a surprising conclusion. I for one was too hasty talking of the **GOK PILES**. In its entirety we concluded Ephesus indeed rivals, albeit in a smaller sense, the Imperial Forum in Rome (I recall Ephesus was, after all, the capital of the Eastern Roman Empire). Ephesus in its totality showed us the grandeur of Greece plus Rome plus the Christian Era. It should never be missed. And the archeologists in a few decades will have restored and rebuilt all those fallen columns.

We reminded each other of what was not in the ruins: the Christian stories, legend or real, of the last days of the Blessed Virgin Mary, St. John's caring for her in her last days, and the preaching of no less than St. Paul. I repeat a folk tale regarding St. Paul: while he preached Christianity, a local jeweler who made Artemis cult statues provoked the audience shouting, "The Ephesus of Artemis is great; the Ephesus of Artemis is Supreme." It was a hard row to hoe. How does Paul compete with you know what? A joke.

In sum, Ephesus is an incredible place, an important place, the "capital" of Rome in the East in the days of empire. But one can see the site is indeed a "work in progress." We admired Turkey for the effort. Princess was wise to include the site in the itinerary.

CANTO VI

ISTANBUL

Here are my on – board notes for the Introduction; I summarized.

7th century B.C.: the city was founded by the Greeks and called Byzantium.

4th century A.D.: the capital of the Roman Empire was transferred here by Constantine and it was called Nova Roma. It became Constantinople named after its emperor. It later became Istanbul after the Ottoman Turk victory in 1453.

Istanbul was built on seven hills like Rome; the European side has the Golden Horn. The Galata Bridge links Europe and Asia Minor. The Bosporus separates the European from the Asian side and there is a long suspension bridge.

RELATED POINTS OF HISTORY:

For perspective, note that 3000 B.C. marks the founding of Troy, i.e. the Trojan War of Greek literary fame.

1750 – 1200 B.C. These are the dates for the Hittite Kingdom in Anatolia (Turkey).

658 B.C. Byzantium is founded by Greeks from the Peloponnese, but not really built up; it was a stopping place for Greek colonies heading to the Black Sea!

546 B.C. The Persians invade under Cyrus II.

334 B.C. Alexander the Great of Greece defeats the Persians.

146 B.C. An alliance between Byzantium and Rome takes place. 133 B.C. The king of Pergamum dies and leaves his realm to Rome. Anatolia is annexed by Rome and becomes the Province of Asia.

A.D. 330. Constantine the Great chooses Byzantium as the capital of the Eastern Roman Empire. Asia Minor is widely Christianized at the time, but Rome is still pagan.

A.D. 337. Constantine dies.

A.D. 476. Rome falls; Constantinople becomes even more important in the East until 1453.

1045 A.D. The Seljuk Turks move into Anatolia from the East; Byzantium asks for military help from the West to combat the Moslems, and the result is the first Crusade in 1097.

1204 A.D. Catholic crusaders sack Constantinople's riches.

1453 A.D. Mehmet II captures Constantinople and makes it the capital of his Ottoman Empire.

1520 - 1566. These are the dates for the peak of the Ottoman Empire under Suleiman the Magnificent. But the empire shall continue for many years.

1853 – 1856 A.D. The Crimean War takes place. The English and French fight Russians on the side of the Turks.

1908. Ataturk comes into power. Turkey is allied with Germany during WWI. The Battle of Gallipoli in WW I took place in 1915. The Allies were soundly defeated. (Liam Clancy has a great and classic song about this same event, but from an Australian soldier's point of view.)

1923. This is the foundation of the Turkish Republic. Ataturk rules and reforms: he modernizes, initiates Western dress, the use of the Latin alphabet, and moves the capital to Ankara.

1952. Turkey joins NATO in 1952.

The more notes, the more important the place. I tried to make it interesting and not just a list of dates and happenings. One guy in the audience said, "Who cares Professor? If you finish, we can all go down and enjoy Chef's afternoon tea goodies." Some laughter, some protests. I retorted, "We aim to please. For all those weary of history and such, Istanbul's bazaar is one of the best and most varied in the world. But, ahem, hang on to your purse, your billfold and your documents. You can smoke a hookah, or even buy one, and I understand that they offer several hundred rugs, each with a different pattern. And there's the coffee. Oh, I'll join you in those sweets."

It turns out it was far more, fresh shrimp, breads, you name it. See the photos.

The Royal Princess Chef and Snacks

Sweets for All and a Sweetie

Dinner is just in two hours, so we had to deal with that. We did several "laps" on the promenade deck to prepare, and after another fine dinner did a rare thing, taking in a magic and humor show in the auditorium. Then to bed before the amazing entrance to Istanbul that all would see. Warning: Istanbul is overwhelming, but sorry, someone had to see it. To make it easier, I'll list the places and the reader can pick and choose according to his/ her stamina for history.

The Harbor; Royal Princess Coming In
The Blue Mosque
Hagia Sophia
Topkapki Palace
Lunch on board
Chora Church and Mosaics
The Old City and its Wall
The Basilica Cistern
The finale and well deserved: the Sulimaniye Mosque

We did this in one day! Some RP travelers cut out, went to the bazaar and then to the entertainment of those guys with funny hats with tassels who twirl in circles. We were about that dizzy after the Mosques. Coming up are snippets of each of the sights, impossible to do from pre – on deck lecture. Each to his own with the Michelin Guide or the on-shore guides supplied by Princess.

The Royal Princess coming in and first view of the Blue Mosque and Hagia Sophia.

Istanbul, the Blue Mosque and Sancta Sophia

THE BLUE MOSQUE.

It was done in the 17th century by Sultan Ahmet. It has six minarets or call to prayer towers; it once had seven but one was given to Mecca so as to not outdo the birthplace of Mohammed. It boasts 21,000 blue tiles in flower and geometric designs along with four fluted pillars; carpets and cupola. Each year caravans to Mecca leave from here.

Closeup, the Blue Mosque

There were more minarets from outside and the Egyptian Obelisk. This area was the original hippodrome of Byzantium built by the Roman Emperor Septum Severus in 203 A.D. and was remodeled by Emperor Constantine in 326 A.D. It had a stadium, circus, meeting place for politicians, games, races, a capacity for 100,000 spectators, chariots, etc. The obelisk dates from 1500 B.C. and was from Karnack in ancient Egypt. It was brought by Roman Emperor Theodosius to Istanbul in A.D. 390. The obelisk has hieroglyphics on the Egyptian part, but the base has carved scenes of Emperor Theodosius and his empress watching races in the Hippodrome.

High above, the stained glass "blue" windows which give the place its name.

Stained glass windows of the Blue Mosque

ON TO THE HAGIA SOPHIA.

This was the first Christian Basilica built by Roman Emperor Constantine in 325. It burned down later. In 532 A.D. it was rebuilt by Emperor Justinian, dedicated to the "Holy Wisdom of God" or Hagia Sophia. The red bricks on the dome are from the isle of Rhodes, the red columns from Rome, the silver and gold work were from Ephesus, the white marble from Marmara Isles, and the yellow marble from Africa. Ceiling and domes were all done in mosaic. When Emperor Justinian saw it finished, he proclaimed, "Oh Solomon, I have surpassed you!"

There were earthquakes and it was plundered by crusaders in 1204.

In 1453 it was converted into a mosque and four minarets were added.
In the 19th century it was restored.

In 1935 it was converted into a museum. The cupola is higher than that of the Blue Mosque.

It is much older, is more worn, and has been through more. We concluded that for History, it is most important, but the Blue Mosque takes your breath away! Here is the exterior view of Hagia Sophia from the Blue Mosque:

The Great Hagia Sophia from the Blue Mosque

There are many mosaics from the Byzantine Era, most of them in need of repair; most impressive was that of the Virgin Mary in the apse of Hagia Sophia.

Mosaic of the Virgin from the Apse of Hagia Sophia

It was dim inside; the mosaics were far, far above us and as mentioned, most showing the wear and tear of centuries. My photos do not due them justice, nor the multi- marbled floor. The Vatican, from what seemed eons ago, sports floors which were more impressive. Go figure, 300 A.D. to 1500 A.D.

TOPKAPI PALACE: RESIDENCE OF THE SULTANS AND THE HAREM - THE SERAGLIO * Check Mozart's Opera!

This was the ancient residence of the Ottoman sultans, built by Mehmet II the conqueror of Istanbul in 1462, but added to by successive sultans. Only the sultan could go on horseback through the main gate. The harem was set apart; the sultan's apartment (and that of his wives and concubines) was here. The Sultan could have four wives and innumerable concubines; much palace intrigue existed to see which wife or concubine could first produce a male heir and then assure his accession to the throne. The Palace was amazing as were its riches; I document with many photos. The Moslem world indeed can be proud.

The Entrance with Arabic Script, Topkapi Palace

The Topkapi dagger, a gift from the sultan to the ruler of Iran who died, so it was returned to the sultan.

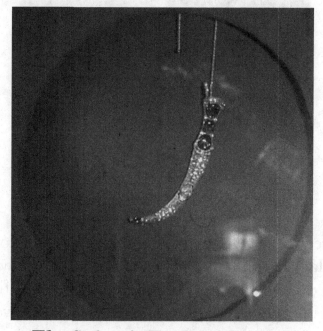

The Sultan's Topkapi Dagger

Not pictured is the Holiday Throne, gold plates and peridots; the Sultan sat here on holidays and received greetings. Imagine.

When we saw what was next, the Imperial (sultan's) armor, Amy and I recalled the stupendous armor rooms in Spain, and I the same in the Museum of Art in New York. This matches them.

The Sultan's Armor

I hope the reader can forgive me for all these photos, more than I salvaged from Hagia Sophia, but my excuse is we in the western world do not have a chance to see all that made up an empire in its time comparable to much of what one sees in Spain, France, Germany or even England.

An important note: in 1570 the Western Christian Alliance of countries battled the Ottoman Empire (Turks) at the Battle of Lepanto, and won! Young Miguel de Cervantes ("Don Quixote de la Mancha") fought in the battle, lost use of one arm thus becoming "El Manco de Lepanto.")

I conclude with this image of the entrance to the Sacred Relics Rooms (of Mohammed). I close with this photo due to the Moslem practice of using script from the Kuran as well as Arabic tile as their choice. We could only recall the Alhambra in Spain from our AT trip a few years ago.

Entrance to the Relics Room of Mohammed

Oh, by the way, the Harem was closed!

THE CHORA CHURCH

It is on the outskirts of old Istanbul and has the best-preserved Mosaics from the Byzantine period. It was built before Roman Emperor Theodosius built the old city walls in 413 A.D. There were earthquakes, etc. The present church is from 12th and 13th centuries. Its most famous mosaic is that of Jesus Pantocrator: he rises as Pantocrator. This image was copied for centuries in the West.

Jesus Pantocrator, Recreated throughout Christendom

They claim the "best" of the Chora Mosaics is the "dormition" of Mary. It is debatable; we remembered Jesus. Mary lies in her death bed, behind the bed Jesus rises with the child in his arms symbolizing the soul of his mother; saints surround the bed, two angels on the right; Anne, Elizabeth and Mary Magdalene stand.

After the Chora, we boarded a tour bus and drove by the old city walls built by Theosodian in 400 A.D. No photos. But then a highlight for movie buffs was the Ilus Cistern from Roman times and with Corinthian capitals. Why? My favorite actor Sean Connery and in my humble view, his best of the series, "From Russia with Love," was filmed here. It provided water for the city.

THE SULIMANIYE MOSQUE - 1550

Last but far from least in this dizzying day was the Sulimaniye Mosque. The architect was Sinan who was used for most buildings by Sulimaniye the Magnificent, 10th Ottoman Sultan. Thousands of people were employed to build it: craftsmen, workers, soldiers, slaves, etc. It was finished in 1557 with 27 columns, 28 domes, four minarets with 10 balconies. The Dome is 47 meters high; the apse faces toward Mecca; the Imam leads prayers from the Sultan's box. There are no galleries or aisles.

The "call to prayer" came from the minarets, formerly sung; it is now often recorded. Loudspeakers were introduced in mosques in the 1930s where they are used by a muezzin for the adhan («call to prayer»), and sometimes for khutbah in Islam. Outdoor loudspeakers, usually mounted on tall minarets, are used five times a day for the call to prayer. Loudspeakers are sometimes also used inside mosques to deliver sermons or for prayer. Electrically amplified adhans have become commonplace in countries such as Turkey and Morocco. One wise guy remarked, "No recording contracts before, huh?"

To the "western ear," the call to prayer can be both mysterious and beautiful; Amy and I found it both. Some Adventurers were disappointed to not hear and see a real person high up the minaret doing the "call." It should happen five times per day.

Ablution fountains are required for spiritual bathing. We also saw them in Spain some years ago both in Córdoba and Granada. Old Mr. Owens from Cincinnati spoke up, "What if you Catholics had to wash your feet before Mass? Arrive early for the best towels."

And finally, a pilgrim bent in prayer toward Mecca. I half way expected to be escorted out of this place (like in the Cathedral of León, Spain, another story in another book), but perhaps Allah was pleased. I was sincere in my prayer, the only time such a thing occurred to me. God has many names.

Pilgrim at Prayer in the Sulimaniye Mosque

Several of us had dinner on deck that night, a once in a lifetime chance to experience the evening lights reflected on the water and all three mosques of Istanbul. Oh, we did hear the "call to prayer" from the recordings and were appreciative even of that. Then, exhausted to bed, a great day ahead.

CANTO VII

RUSSIA – YALTA AND ODESSA

There is a day and night at sea to come. The water of the Black Sea is green and calm, and there is an abundance of Russian shipping. Time out for food: the buffet lunch featured shrimp, crab salad, roast beef, and many chocolate treats. A long walk followed on the promenade deck. I even got on an exercise bike (ha, the only time), and we both climbed into one of the Jacuzzis, and a nap followed.

The following morning it was back "on duty," providing the history of what we were shortly to see around 9 a.m. - the mountains and shoreline of Yalta. My talk (recall Russia is still the USSR and the Berlin Wall is still up):

YALTA – INTRODUCTION

This in 1989 was Russia's most glamorous seaside resort; the Crimean Mountains shelter it from the north winds. Its climate is said to be a Riviera - style climate. It shares the past grandeur of the Tsarist era; the old aristocratic mansions are now government hotels or sanatoria. The 19th century aristocrats wanted their places and Yalta to rival Nice or Cannes. The Czar built his imperial palace at Livadia in the 1860s. Yalta was the place of the 1945 Yalta Conference between Stalin, Churchill and Roosevelt when they agreed on how to split up Europe after the Nazi defeat. Chekov, Tolstoy, Gorky, Tchaikovsky and Rachmaninoff all spent time here. Mark Twain visited in 1867. In 1920 Lenin proclaimed it to be the property of the people.

History:

700 B.C. TO 800 A.D. There were Greek colonies at Yalta with Hellenistic, Roman and Arabic cultures there.

800 - 988 A.D. Slavs migrate and found Kiev. Kiev is later conquered by the Vikings who rule all of central Russia to the 16th century.

1223 - 1480 A.D. Mongol and Tartar invasions come from the Northeast under Genghis Khan. They conquer Russia and Russia pays tribute.

14th century. The Grand Princedom of Muscovy is established. Yalta is owned by the Genoese at this time and will be until the Turks arrive in 1475.

1480 - 1825. Ivan III ends Tartar rule, becomes "Ivan the Terrible" and the first Russian czar in 1547. Later there is a Polish invasion and they are only driven out in 1612. Mikail Romanov is elected czar and the Romanoff dynasty begins. (Yalta is still under the Turks.)

1721. Peter I claims the title of Peter the Great! Catherine II, the Great, widow of Peter I's grandson rules. Russia annexes the Crimea and Yalta.

1812. Napoleon invades but is defeated.

1825 - 1905. Russia loses the Crimean War to France and Britain.

From 1835 – 1856 Czar Alexander VI tries reforms, wants equality between the nobility and the peasants, but fails. He begins to build his imperial palace at Livadia. Yalta becomes a resort for the Russian aristocracy.

1917. The Revolution. Trotsky helps Lenin take power in 1917 - 1919. Everything is nationalized. Yalta belongs to the people.

1924. Constitution of the Soviet Union, one year after Lenin's death. Stalin is in as leader.

1940 - 1945. Germany occupies much of the USSR including the Crimea, but in February, 1945, the Yalta Conference decides the future.

We were moved around in a very comfortable tour bus. One could see low mountains in the background, but the first big site was:

Alupka Palace, 1828 - 1848 (Voronstov's palace)

It was built in the Tudor style. Count Voronstov, mayor and governor of Odessa, built this to rival Livadia and the palace of the Czar.

This tapestry is from the Czarist period. A marvelous artistic look back in history.

Czarist Tapestry from the Alupka Palace, Yalta

In the same room there was a piano. Rachmaninoff played here. He's the one in the movie who went crazy trying to play Piano Concierto n.1.

I do not know her duties but she is resting. More than once we believed we were seeing Marxist Russia.

A Member of the Staff of the Palace

Supposedly the Count was copying the Alhambra (and wanting to better the Czar). See Amy and the terrace of the lions at Alupka made of Carrara marble; these are copies of the lions on Pope Clement XII's tomb in Rome. Our guide emphasizes Voronstav "employed" 40,000 to 80,000 serfs to build this place, "He was richer than the czar!"

The Lions of Alupka Palace

Then we saw the entrance and garden of Livadia Palace, the Czar's summer house in Italian Renaissance Style. In modern times it was famous for the Yalta Conference with Stalin the host, Churchill and Franklin D. Roosevelt. They supposedly discussed how they would divide up Europe after the war. There was a plaque in Russian language about the Palace and the 1945 meeting. The meeting room was very simple in décor.

After that came the Russian – style treat: a big lunch and then Russian folk dancing in the stylish tourist hotel in Yalta. The show was "folklore" with Crimean song and dance. The banquet featured generous "doses" of vodka accompanied by caviar, fish, borsht, stew, wine, and ice cream.

Everyone was quite jovial after that and enjoyed this slice of Marxist Russia. The odd thing was in this "luxury" hotel, all the lights were turned out before and after the show.

Folk Dancing, Borsht, Vodka and Caviar, Yalta Hotel

Rested and now ready for naps, the tour bus took us to Yalta harbor and departure. There was an old Russian Orthodox church with a mushroom tower in the distance but it was not on the tour. We were glad to be back aboard and on our way to the important city of Odessa, on the Black Sea of Crimea.

ODESSA AND SURPRISES

Before I go on, I want to say tourism was very controlled, regimented; there was no contact at all with Russian people allowed. Just the guide.

Here are my notes of introduction from on deck as we slowly moved into the dock. 1989.

Odessa - "Pearl of the Black Sea"

Odessa is Ukraine's third largest city of one million and is located on the northwest corner of the Black Sea; it was built at the behest of Catherine the Great in the 18th century. It had its heyday as a cultural center in Russia. Pushkin spent one year in exile here in 1823; Gorky was here as a port worker in 1896, and Gogol wrote here. Ethnic population is made up of Ukrainian Russians, Greeks, Bulgarians and Jews.

Odessa was a free port under the Czars and was open to the West. The first stirrings of the Bolshevik revolution were here with the mutineers on the Battleship "Potemkin" in 1905 when the dockworkers joined in the strike.

Today its major elements are petrol refining, shipping, industry, mud baths for resorts, spas and sanatoria.

The history is similar to Yalta: Rule was by Greeks, Slavs, Tartars, Turks and finally Russians in 1791 during the era of Catherine the Great.

In 1801 a Frenchman, the Duc de Richelieu, is named mayor of Odessa by Alexander 1 and the city flourishes.

1814 - 1849. Odessa is a free port, its major product grain from the Ukraine.

1854. An Anglo - French fleet bombards Odessa. The Crimean War begins.

1905. Sailors and workers revolt and fail. There is suppression and a pogrom against the Jews. 13 per cent of the population flees.

1917 - 20. There is civil war, a time of great suffering, starvation.

1941. There is a 69-day siege by the German troops, local resistance moves to the underground catacombs, Germany controls Odessa until 1944.

1944. The city is freed and named "hero city" in the USSR.

1989. There is industry, the port, oil, and the whaling fleet of USSR.

We saw the Monument to the sailors of the "Potemkin," the abortive revolt of 1905, then the monument to Puskin of 1888 on Primorsky Blvd. My picture is depressing.

Another depressing but revealing moment of Marxism in Odessa in 1989 was this building, opposite the famed Opera House. We surmised you had to go by it to get to the Opera House. Amy whispered, "We have our slums and bad sections of towns at home, too." "In front of the Opera House?" Food for thought. Mike, the farmer's son, was interested in the Russian tractor and trailer; their version of the John Deere with cab! Ha ha.

The Russian Tractor

On to better things: the side and front of the Opera House, 1884 - 1887, one of best in Europe. Built on classic baroque lines imitating the Vienna Opera House and the Dresden Court Theater. Scenes from Shakespearian plays adorn the ceiling. We were not allowed to go inside and form our own opinion.

The Odessa Opera House

One of the lighter and better moments of Odessa was a surprise encounter with Russian schoolchildren who actually smiled. One New Yorker in our group remarked, "Oi, we could be in Brooklyn."

Students in Odessa

"Official Russia" followed with the Party Headquarters. At least we saw the front – red banner with Marx, Engles and Lenin - and a public building on our 40-minute unscheduled stop. I add, we were not scheduled for an inside visit.

Communist Party Headquarters, Odessa

This was when things got dicey. Forty minutes, hmm. I decided to leave the group (a definite no – no) when I spotted the cupula of what had to be the major Russian Orthodox church in Odessa. It was only a five-minute walk from the group. Amy shook her head "no," but it was too late. I've said before I am impulsive at times (aha again), with rewards in travel from not being with the group. Acting like I belonged (ha!) I walked in the entrance and was surprised; it was in the middle of a service. One photo (I could have been arrested) suffices.

Russian Orthodox Service

The "official tour" was waiting a few blocks away, shown the front of a "modern" Russian department store, but not invited to go inside. My question: what was on the second floor? And are customers queuing up?

Odessa Department Store

We did see the outside of the Odessa Cathedral. Here is a quick shot of Uspensky (Assumption) Cathedral, one of the few churches left in Odessa. Russo - Byzantine style from 1855 - 69. There were five domes and a 150 ft. bell tower. Not on the tour. But as Amy said, "Think what we might have seen." That was our conclusion as we later sailed out of Odessa.

Odessa Cathedral, Outside

The final stop and with no hurry was to see the Childrens' Guard at the "Heroes" monument dedicated to the young sailors who defended Odessa from the Nazis. Changing of the guard with the goose step.

Childrens' Guard, Heroes Monument

This then is the view, limited but very impressive, of Odessa in the Crimea in 1989. We all were glad to be back aboard Princess and then to sail out of the harbor from what some called a depressing experience.

I think that more than depressing, it was eye – opening. The Cold War really had gone on since 1945 with the Russian division and blockade between East and west Germany (old timers on board reminded us of President Harry Truman and the Berlin Airlift via DC 3s which ferried supplies into west Berlin), then forty years of division with the West. We had a taste of Czarist Russia and its beauty (albeit, at the cost of the peasants and the pleasures of the Czars and Count Vorontsov), and now "late" Russian life in its "resort" "political" cities.

I'm thinking, for the reader and certainly for the Adventurers and RP passengers, the above paragraphs may bring unnecessary memories of perhaps the gloomy times in Yalta and Odessa, but perhaps I protest too much. That experience was invaluable and indeed rare for a western traveler in those times. And one got an inkling of the best of Czarist and (lesser so) Marxist times.

I do admit to a sigh of relief as we sailed outside of Odessa.

Regardless, Princess put on the dog that night to make us forget our bleak assessment of Yalta and Odessa: drinks, escargot, French onion soup, frog legs, sirloin steak, parfait a la Gran Marnier, petit fours. That wearied us enough and it was early to bed to prepare for our departure from the Black Sea and on to Mykonos and Delos.

CANTO VIII

THE BOSPHOROUS STRAIT - ON BOARD THE PRINCESS – ON TO MYKONOS AND DELOS

The next morning I had a new experience – lox and bagels for breakfast - and then was on deck using the deck speakers to tell of the sights of our departure from the Black Sea and Russia and seeing once again the shore from the Bosporos – first, Mehmet's great castle – fortress (matching any we had seen in Spain!). He built it prior to the last battle when he conquered Constantinople in 1453.

Mehmet's Fortress, Istanbul

Next came the bridge over the Bosporus (built by the Japanese) connecting Europe and Asia at Istanbul. Hmm. The Japanese did the one in Lisbon as well.

Bridge Over the Bosporos, Europe – Asia Minor

And finally, a nostalgic view of Istanbul and the Blue Mosque before the Aegean and the Cyclades - Mykonos and Delos.

Leaving the Bosporos, Istanbul and the Blue Mosque

With two days to Mykonos and Delos in the Aegean I've chosen Canto VIII as "catch up" of matters between AT and RP and life on board. First thing was a long session with Captain Johansen and Sally Reynolds assessing the trip so far. We did it over the Chef's terrific breakfast treats and fine coffee.

The Captain spoke first, "Mike, I think it has been great. Royal Princess passengers tend to prefer the on-board comforts, stops at the French Riviera or the "biggies" of Europe. All this history, ancient and modern, has been good for them. Thank you for informing us, entertaining us, and sometimes boring us. Just kidding!"

Sally added, "We've really hit it on the head this time. Life is not all comfortable and afternoon tea – but your humor, I'm thinking the GOK PILES, smoothed out a rough road. If you ever need another job, we have other ships. And Amy mainly stayed out of my hair but has an eagle eye for a shore stop that might not work or need improving. Thanks to you both."

Amy said, "Our turn. It is to RP's credit for this amazing itinerary. And someone, maybe those old Greek or Roman gods, have been smiling on us. No war, no revolution, all has been calm, and everyone will go home much the wiser! It certainly has been a departure from birds and beasts on our usual AT expeditions. Like someone said, maybe marble, silver and gold animals have a charm of their own!"

I said, "More to come, much more. Delos, Athens and Sounion for the history buffs, and Mykonos for the partiers. Thank you both again. Oh, GOK PILES AHEAD!"

Much laughter with an agreement to repeat the meeting just before docking at Naples in a few days.

So, there were two full days at sea enjoying the comforts of capitalistic (I want to contrast to the Marxist gloominess some adventurers are still talking about) - tourism – life aboard Princess.

I can't include all the "at ease" photos, but here we go with some highlights. I will just say that no passenger ever needs to be bored on board! Between constant food venues from snacks to fine dining, a well-supplied bar on the Lido Deck, exercise rooms, the Promenade deck, and all the entertainment venues (movie theater, night club with eats and entertainment, and a small casino) we have, uh, happy campers. There is a library as well, although I thought it was sparsely used whenever I passed by.

One photo suffices to see our room. Extremely comfortable, say no more.

Amy, Our Room, Princess

I have not talked about any of the ship's features below for several reasons. The goal for AT was culture and history, albeit enjoying Princesses' hospitality. I'm limited on images as it is to avoid this book costing a fortune. Travelers had their own few hundred photo souvenirs.

1. Amy on Lido deck for breakfast
2. Lido deck, pool and Jacuzzi
3. Sun deck, Lido
4. Top deck and lap pool
5. Top deck and exercise room and stack
6. The stack, flags (Turkey as well) and radar towers
7. Another of jacuzzi and pools
8. Amy in the jacuzzi
9. The Horizon Lounge again

This is the gangway we all used for on shore.

The Gangway, Princess

This is a favorite couple from Arkansas, Royal Princess travelers that we had occasion to talk to, have a drink and a meal or two and compare RP and AT.

Mike, Amy, Arkansas Couple

The "business" part of top deck – communication antennae, flags and the full blast of the engines propelling the ship.

Stacks and Flags, the Princess

And finally, Amy acting like a tourist and enjoying the hot water jacuzzi. I am in swim suit with her but someone had to do the photo. Who, I surmise, would the curious reader rather see?

Amy, the Jacuzzi, Princess

I think I've shown the food earlier; yes, RP does best AT in this category. I've never eaten such delicacies, even day after day, anytime, anywhere!

CANTO IX

GREECE – THE CYCLADES ISLANDS: DELOS AND MYKONOS

Map of Ancient Greece, the Cyclades

We first arrived to Mykonos, with Delos nearby. Here are some tidbits from the on – board introduction. For history and indeed scholars of Western Civilization Delos is one of (pardon Nebraska baseball talk) the "big hitters." I only had studied a smattering of this time and part of the world, never studied Greek language, but had friends in graduate school who were steeped in the Classics. That was one reason Rome and Greece would be so important on the trip. We indeed thought it would an "education" for all, and it was, ten times over! The Jesuits in college did require us to read "The Dialogues of Plato" (I scraped by with a low C), and read "The Iliad" and the "Odyssey" and the "Aeneid". More important to me was "El Poema del Cid" and the "Lusiads," Spain and Portugal's versions of the epic tradition inherited from Greece and Rome.

DELOS

In the Aegean islands, Delos is the hub of the Cyclades a "circle" of islands around sacred Delos. Homer spoke of it as the "wine, dark sea." Barren and haunting. Its history:

1300 B.C. Myceneans from the Greek mainland dominated the Aegean.

776 - 500 BC. The first Olympic Games were held in 776 B.C. Then the Greeks began expansion. Delos known as Phoebus Apollo's (The Sun God's) birthplace becomes the major religious shrine. Is is their "church."

500 - 31 B.C. The Persian Wars begin. Persians conquer the Cyclades in 490 B.C., land at Marathon and are defeated by the Athenians. Here's where the LEGEND begins. Supposedly a Greek named Philippedes saw the remaining Persian ships leave, change course and head to Athens, surmising an attack on the city. So, our hero, beginning at Marathon, the site of the Greek victory, ran all the way to Athens to warn them of a possible Persian attack. He entered the assembly hall, made his announcement and dropped dead. Hmm. 26 miles plus, no wonder. The

legend is recounted in endless books, paintings and such. It has been proclaimed, indeed, legend. Who knows!

The Greeks regain the Aegean Sea at the naval battle of Salamis in 480 B.C.

Athens forms the Delian League (Delos and islands) and Delos becomes part of the Athenian Empire.

454 B.C. The Delos treasure is transferred to Athens by Pericles.

431 - 404. The Peloponnesian War takes place between Athens and Sparta.

336 B.C. Alexander the Great of Macedonia rules Greece; Delos is a free port.

88 B.C. King Mithridates of Asia Minor sacks Delos.

31 B.C. All of Greece is incorporated into the Roman Empire.

336 A.D. to 1832: Epidemics, Byzantine Wars, and the Turks weaken the islands.

1832: Greece gains independence from the Ottomans; Bavarian Prince Otto becomes the first King. The Cyclades are now part of Greece.

DELOS – THE "POMPEII" OF GREECE

It was the birthplace of the great god Apollo (the Sun God). I interject a personal note: the sun god becomes part of the beautiful Brazilian movie, "Black Orpheus," a staple of life for students of Brazil. Rulers, warriors and pilgrims came to consult its oracle (the second most important in Greece after Delphi, considered by the ancient Greeks to be the center of the world and the oracle Pthyia). Delos is located between Asia Minor and Greece.

There was a huge slave market, ten thousand sold in single day. I limit the images because this place, thousands of years old, matched and put in the shade the other **GOK PILES** we had seen (some in Rome, some in Crete). The Classics Majors will never pardon me.

Royal Princess at anchor in the bay outside Mykonos

Princess at Mykonos

With Princess docked off shore from Mykonos and offering shuttles to that busy tourist center, a few of us, the more curious, found our way to Delos via the local ferry and were greeted by a general view of the ruins.

Overview, Delos

The GOK PILE defense rests its case.

We saw the Stoibadeion or temple of Dionysus, pardon me, The Party God known as Bacchus in Roman times. An outsize phallus was his symbol! The slide shows a side view of testicles and broken – off phallus, 300 B.C. The relief is of Dionysus and the Maenads or a small Silenus and Pan, partiers of those times. Not seen is the front relief of a cock's (rooster's) body but the neck up is an oversized phallus!

Dionysius Stone, Delos

The terrace of the lions, 7th century B.C. One of the lions is at the arsenal in Venice. This view is facing east, looking at the Sacred Lake where Phoebus Apollo was born.

Terrace of the Lions, Delos

We saw the columns of the Poseidoniasts. Built by the merchants and shop owners from Beirut, worshipers of Neptune (Poseidon). Then came the House of Dionysus (with a mosaic of Dionysus seated on a panther).

We wondered why they had not reconstructed the Theater (as in Rome, Ephesus and even tiny Crete). Here it is from the Hellenistic Period, with a capacity of 5000.

The Theater, Delos

There are a few surviving mosaics. One was a mosaic floor is in what they call the House of the Dolphins, a dolphin in harness driven by a winged cupid. One recalls Crete.

And an outstanding mosaic completes that specific experience: The House of the Masks. 2nd.century B.C. A dancing Silen (we missed the best: Dionysus on the cat.)

House of the Mask Mosaics, Delos

Temple of Isis

This was the only standing or rebuilt structure that we had really expected to see (like in Rome) but Greece would outdo itself later in Athens.

Rebuilt Temple, Delos

At the base of one of many columns on Delos: a bull's head and grapes. These were seen throughout Delos. Books have been written on bulls, bull jumping, and how it all ended in Spain (and the Americas) with the modern "corrida de toros."

Bull's Head, Delos

After all the "bull," it was time to take our small ferry back to the ship. My graduate school Classics' buddies would have been proud of us. We had the p.m. in Mykonos, on the "circuit" of tourist stops in the Cyclades.

MYKONOS

It is a granite island, typical of the Cyclades, arid, windswept, cubed houses, windmills, chapels.

13th - 18th century A.D. Mykonos is in the hands of the Venetians who brought Roman Catholicism; there were pirates, both Berber and Christian.

The wind is important, and the narrow streets were to help cut off the winds from houses. Over 300 chapels were built as votive offerings by the sailors, their domes in colors. The houses are whitewashed.

The Royal Princess. Lifeboats ready to ferry to Mykonos

Princess Boats to Mykonos

Amy and the Quay at Mykonos

The Wharf at Mykonos

The Greek Orthodox priest and the taxi driver. No free lunch for the former.

The Orthodox Priest and the Taxi Driver.

Amy and One of the Famous Island Windmills

Amy and the Windmill at Mykonos

A Prize-Winning Image – the Royal Princess Seen from the Windmill.

The Royal Princess Through the Windmill

A Tiny Greek Orthodox chapel.

Mykonos, the Orthodox Chapel and View

We found a tiny bar back at the quay, admired the "catch of the day," a glass enclosed case with lobsters, and best of all, heard wonderful classical guitar music albeit recorded, in the bar. Then it was back aboard ship and the travel to Athens! My last image the wonderful windmills surrounding the quay.

The Windmills, Mykonos Departure

CANTO X
ATHENS AND SOUNION

My lecture on deck as we headed into the port of Piraeus of Athens was much shorter than these notes. As they used to say in all those Liberal Arts Colleges, Athens is the foundation and key to "Western Civilization." And it also is the key to history all through the Aegean and Mediterranean Oceans. Consider the material to come a "reference shelf" to what we saw. I've relented to history and tourism. You will need the map of Ancient Greece:

Reprise, Map of Ancient Greece, to Athens

ATHENS - HISTORY AND PRELUDE TO ROME AND MODERN EUROPE

Today in 1989 it is a city of over 3 million in a country of 9 million.

2000 - 776 B.C. The Achaeans, the Aeolians and the Ionians from the North settle the Greek mainland.

1400 - 1340 B.C. The Siege of Troy. In Literature, "The Iliad." Homer.

1100 B.C. Dorians invade and destroy Mycenaean culture.

776 B.C. First record of the Olympic Games

500 B.C. Athens, Sparta, Thebes and the wars. All types of government, great literature, law, statesmen and philosophers.

490 B.C. The Athenians defeat Darius the Persian at Marathon.

480 B.C. The Greeks hold up the Persians under Xerxes at Thermopylae while Athens is evacuated. Xerxes plunders Athens.

480 B.C. The Greek fleet defeats the Persians at Salamis.

479 B.C. Greek independence is assured, the Persians are whipped.

431 - 407 BC. Athens' Golden Age under Pericles. The Parthenon is built.

The Peloponnesian War: Athens and Sparta; Sparta wins with help of Persia.

322 B.C. Macedonia rises; Phillip II and Alexander the Great.

262 B.C. Macedonia occupies Athens; Athens in decline.

146 B.C. Macedonia becomes a Roman province.

86 B.C. Roman General Sulla sacks Athens, takes many treasures to Rome.

50 A.D. St. Paul comes, Christianity takes root in Greece.

326 - 1204: The time of the Byzantine Empire from Constantinople (originally a Greek colonial town); Athens in obscurity.

529 A.D. Roman Emperor Justinian closes the last pagan temples in Athens and the Athens School of Philosophy.

Athens is ruled successively by the Burgundians, Catalonia, Florence and finally the Turks in 1456.

1466. The Venetians take Athens, then the Turks, Venetians again in 1687 and the bombardment damages the Parthenon. Then Dark ages of Athens under Ottoman rule follow.

1834. Greek Independence (influence of Lord Byron and letters

and the alliance of Britain.) Athens is the new capital; the ruler is King Otto of Bavaria.

1941 - 1944. Nazi Occupation. Freed in 1944.

1947 - 1949. Civil War in Greece, power struggle. Communists are defeated and Constantine is named King.

1974. Military dictatorship and King Constantine is out and in exile.

Presently: democracy back in.

Once again, the more important, the more details. I did not and could not rattle off this list in the talk on deck, but not one item is unimportant. That is, important for anyone who wants to understand the immense value of Greece in its day. Of course, Rome and the Empire followed.

HIGHLIGHTS OF ANCIENT ATHENS

I mentioned that fans of mythology would have to explain to everyone else this "who's who" of Greek and Athenian religious and cultural life.

Legend: Poseidon (God of the sea) and Athena (Goddess of wisdom) were rivals in their miracles for aiding the first Athenians.

Erechtheos a descendant of Creops established the cult of Athena (the Olive, the Owl); we saw the palace of Erechtheos on the Acropolis.

Pericles: a great statesman, reconstructed Athens after the Persian Wars, built the Acropolis: The Propylaia, the Parthenon, the Erechtheion and the Temple of Athena Nike (Victory).

The Death of Socrates (symbolic decline of Athens): 399 B.C.

Demosthenes: famous orator prior to the Macedonian War

The Hellenistic Period: began with the death of Alexander the Great of Macedonia in 323 B.C.

86 B.C. Roman general Sulla captures Athens and Rome takes over, but intellectually, Athens "rules" over Rome; sons of famous Romans study in Athens; a roman temple is built on the Acropolis; the Roman Odeon in the old Greek "agora."

2nd century A.D. Roman Emperor Hadrian loved Athens and built his Temple of Zeus below and the arch.

Princess did well in this morass of western tourism; we docked at the major port of Piraeus, then got on the tour bus on a freeway to Athens. The bus whisked us through the main modern city highlighting some iconic views of Greece, then the climb to the Parthenon and history relived.

Our Tourism through the lower city: we passed by Hadrian's Arch, The Temple of Zeus, past diverse government buildings, the library, and the university. The palace guards were a hoot with their uniforms and tasseled shoes. Another important modern view was that of the original Olympic Stadium now of course modernized and a monument in itself.

Then it was on to the major event: the Acropolis.

We had a good tour guide on the Acropolis, impressive for its size and height. Massive and full of tourists like us. There was a long steep walkway to the entrance, the Temple of Victory on the right, then THE PARTHENON and TEMPLE OF ATHENA, the Caryatid women forming the columns. Most of the original statues were either destroyed or are in the Athens or British Museums! [4]

The history of the place, the great names and ideas, the plays presented, make for a special environment. The guide's lecture was long and we rushed to get around for pictures and looks. Here are the images.

---

[4] Editor's note: as I write this in 2023 the British Museum is still arguing; the Greeks want the statues from the Parthenon frieze returned to Greece.

The Academy of Athens, the major research center of the nation with an amazing history unlike anywhere else. It is a major government building; statues of Plato and Socrates below and Athena and Apollo are on the pedestals.

The Academy of Athens

The guards in front of the Syntagma Square; we saw the guard changing ceremony in front of the Parliament and the Tomb of the Unknown Soldier.

Syntagma Square. The Greek Guards

The Modern Olympic Stadium of Athens

It was a racecourse built in 330 B.C. by an Athenian statesman Lykourgos for the Panathenaic Games; it was rebuilt by Roman Senator Herodes Atticus in 144 A.D., eventually with 50,000 capacity, later abandoned, and finally, later it became the site of the first modern Olympics in 1870. This is the "new" Panathenaic Stadium of 1980, all in marble, based on the site of the original of 1896, the first Modern Olympic Games, but based on the games of the Panathenaea. Site of the Athens Classic Marathon.

The Modern Olympic Stadium, Athens

On to the "piéce de résistance the" ACROPOLIS!

The Stairway to the Acropolis, Victory Temple

DETAILS AND HISTORY OF THE ACROPOLIS ITSELF

1. The word means "upper town." It is 156 meters high. All the principal buildings are of pen telic marble and are from the age of Pericles, 5th century B.C.

2. The Propylaea. The "gate" to the Acropolis. It originally had the statue of Athena Promachos: 30 feet high and in front of the Propylaea, halfway between the Erectheion and the Parthenon. A warrior figure, in bronze by Pheidias, commemorated the Athenian victory over the Persians.

3. The Parthenon. Doric in style, built at the time of Pericles. The huge Athena statue of gold and bronze was inside the Parthenon in the sanctuary (goddess of wisdom among other attributes, her symbol, the owl). Pheidias also did the sculptures on the Parthenon, all the friezes, all painted in those days. This Athena statue was taken to Constantinople in the Byzantine period and later was destroyed by the crusaders in 1203. The Parthenon was made into an Orthodox church for about 800 years; later it was plundered by the Franks, made into a Roman rite church, St. Mary's of Athens, later into a mosque by the Turks with a minaret at the SW corner. In 1687 the Venetians attacked the Ottomans in Athens, and the bombardment destroyed sculptures and roof of the Parthenon. During the time of the Turkish control, a certain Lord Elgin personally "sacked" the Parthenon for art with phony permission from the Turks, but came upon hard times and had to sell it to the British Museum. It remains there today.

The Parthenon, 1

The original Parthenon had 46 fluted columns, painted friezes (most of the originals are now in the British Museum, including the Birth of Athena scene). The British Museum has 16 scenes in all; one is in the Louvre and several are in the Acropolis Museum.

This indecorous photo owes itself to the desire to replicate such a one from Classics scholar and traveler and "mentor" in graduate school, Dan Hayes.

The Parthenon, Mike Reclined

The original Athena statue inside the Parthenon is estimated to have had one ton of gold. (It was hauled off to Constantinople and later destroyed by overzealous Crusaders.) Another great frieze of the Parthenon with the theme of the parade of the festival of Athena is also in the British Museum. A reproduction.

The Athena Statue Recreated

The Temple of Athena Nike. The temple of Poseidon – Erectheus ancient king of Athens is on one end, the Temple of Athena with the Caryatid female columns is on the other. The Erechtheionis is of Doric and Ionic architecture from 407 B.C. One figure on the Porch of the Caryatids is in the British Museum.

Temple of Athena – Nike, the Caryatids

There is a legend relating events back to our short visit at Crete: Theseus's father, old Aegeus, jumped off the Acropolis from this spot when he saw the black sail of Theseus (instead of the white) returning from Crete and his battle with the Minotaur.

I add the prize winner on the trip for **GOK PILES.** What is the saying, "One person's trash is another person's treasure." Literally! The Greeks and the English are still fighting over this stuff. The fallen parts of the Parthenon to be rebuilt.

The Parthenon's GOK PILE

Next, down the hill from the Acropolis is the Odeon Theater of Herod Atticus. He was a Greek patron of Roman origin who built the Odeon in memory of his Roman wife in 161 B.C. He became a consul and senator of Rome. It was originally a steep-sloped theater with a three-story stone front wall and a wooden roof made of expensive cedar of Lebanon timber. It was used as a venue for music concerts with a capacity of 5,000. It lasted intact until it was destroyed and left in ruins in AD 267. The audience stands and the orchestra (stage) were restored using Pentelic marble in the 1950s. Since then, it has been the main venue of the Athens Festival, which runs from May through October each year, featuring a variety of acclaimed Greek as well as international performances, among them María Callas.

The Theater of Herod Atticus

Other major monuments of ancient Athens below the Acropolis:

1. Hadrian's Arch. It has a Corinthian gate in pen telic marble. 131 - 132 AD. It separated the Greek city and its main street, the Placa, from the new Roman city.

2. The Temple of Zeus. Started by the Greeks as early as 6th century B.C. It was finished by Hadrian in 132 A.D.

3. The Theater of Dionysus (or Theatre of Dionysos, Greek: Θέατρο του Διονύσου) is an ancient Greek theatre in Athens. 6th century B.C. It is built on the south slope of the Acropolis hill, originally part of the sanctuary of Dionysus Eleuthereus (Dionysus the Liberator). The first orchestra terrace was constructed on the site around the mid- to late-sixth century BC, where it hosted the City Dionysia. The theatre reached its fullest extent in the fourth century BC under the epistates of Lycurgus when it would have had a capacity of up to 25,000, and was in continuous use down to the Roman Period. The theatre then fell into decay in the Byzantine era and was not identified, excavated and restored to its current condition until the nineteenth century. (This paragraph is taken from Wiki research sources.)

The great plays were performed here. Theater began with the festivals dedicated to Dionysus (Under the Romans, Bacchus, god of assorted pleasures and wine). But in 5th century B.C. classical dramas were performed here: Aeschylus, Sophocles' "Oedipus Rex," Euripides'"Medea," and Aristophanes' "The Wasps." The theater was used in the 4th century as well, seating for 12,000.

There was a short time for shopping for all of us at stores in the city center and some irate RP and AT folks at being "fleeced" (ah the legend still goes on, recalling from Greek Literature and Mythology, Jason and the Argonauts in search of THE GOLDEN FLEECE. Wiki)

The Golden Fleece

CAPE SOUNION AND THE TEMPLE OF POSEIDON

After Athens, we did a long drive on a coastal beach, past recreational areas for Athenians to Cape Sounion, a site of an impressive colonnaded temple dedicated to Poseidon (Neptune), this on the southernmost point of Attica.

"The Temple of Poseidon is an ancient Greek Temple on Cape Sounion, Greece, dedicated to the god Poseidon (Neptune for the Romans). There is evidence of the establishment of sanctuaries on the cape from as early as the 11th century BC. Sounion's most prominent temples, the Temple of Athena and the Temple of Poseidon, are however not believed to have been built until about 700 BC, and their kouroi (freestanding Greek statues of young men) date from about one hundred years later. The material and size of the offerings at the Temple of Poseidon indicate that it was likely frequented by members of the elite and the aristocratic class. (Wiki)

Temple of Poseidon, Sounion

"The Greeks considered Poseidon to be the "master of the sea". Given the importance to Athens of trade by sea and the significance of its navy in its creation and survival during the fifth century, Poseidon was of a particular relevance and value to the Athenians. (Wiki)

I close with an image of Amy contemplating in wonder what we had seen in Delos and now Athens and Cape Sounion and how blessed we were to see all this in good times. And the people and ships that must have passed this Cape and the History that happened!

Contemplating Cape Sounion

THE DENOUEMENT - The Last Days, Naples and Home

After Cape Sounion, the Royal Princess sailed through the rest of that day and night and docked at Naples early the next morning. We enjoyed the last day on the ship and a final farewell drink in the Horizon Lounge, recalling the amazing days on board and what we and all the Adventurers had seen, courtesy of a modern cruise ship.

Amy, Last Night on the Princess

This is my photo of Naples harbor, the Royal Princess coming in.

The Royal Princess Docking at Naples

Did I mention I was down with a respiratory cold, like most people on the ship at the end of the trip, so was a bit fuzzy on that final day. But there were things to do and people to see. Before disembarking, Amy and I made a point of saying goodbye to our "Adventurer" friends, old Wonky, the Peixotos, and others, and then we did our good byes to Captain Johansen, purser Jenni, and especially to their excursion coordinator Sally Reynolds and my tech system guy Joe Spivey who had helped me set up for the talks. Amy and I shared our belief that the Partnership between "Adventure Travel" and Royal Princess had not only lived up to expectations, but surpassed them. We bade farewell, walked down the outside staircase of Princess and boarded a tour bus for the five hours to Rome.

The one image worth remembering (but a lousy bus photo) recalled from the bus trip to Rome is when we passed Monte Cassino, the "home" of St. Benedict and Saint Scholastica. We did have a final lunch stop with pasta, lasagna and a red wine, providing me with a nice nap into Rome.

I don't remember much about the hotel in Rome or the next morning preparations to the airport, checking in, waiting for a very early departure from Leonardo da Vinci International Airport on TWA to New York and customs. After that long flight, Amy and I then dragged our posteriors back on to TWA and caught the TWA red eye to Los Angeles and the report to James Morrison of "Adventure Travel." We checked in the Marriott and crashed.

A LONG EPILOGUE

After a late afternoon dinner at the Marriott and ten hours sleep for an exhausted couple, Amy and I were ushered into James' office by his second in command Susan Gilliam. Coffee was served and a smiling James Morrison started the "debriefing."

"Well, Michael you scoundrel, and Amy, you AT diplomat, you carried it off! And in a big way. We have been receiving reports, on - going, from the Princess Cruise's public relations department, via phone and print. And they have already faxed us the passenger survey results from on – board questionnaires the middle of last week. And summary remarks from RP's Captain and staff as well. It's all a 'glowing' report. I admit that last March I was skeptical, but if you add all this material to, ahem, our profit margin from one hundred paying "Adventure" travelers on your trip, it leaves no doubt in my mind of the huge success of it all. (The reader needs to know that James Morrison is not one for superlatives, but rather a very pragmatic, nose to the grindstone CEO, so this was unusual.)

"What can I say? It certainly was not AT's standard expedition trip, but it is in a way a 'breath of fresh air' for the company. Times indeed are a changing as ole' Bob Dylan once sang, but I don't think this trip and itinerary can be repeated for a long time. In fact, it might have been a one – time thing. Politics and events in that part of the world are in a state of flux. And you both know, there could have been some unexpected and even dangerous happenings on the trip. But Poseidon indeed protected you on the seas! (Laughter).

"Joe Caufield of Princess Cruises (he and James evidently now are good buddies) already called me and said we both should keep an open mind about any future possibilities of cooperation and partnership. Evidently those 700 RP passengers were pleased and profitable as well. Even if it never happens, that is a very good conclusion to this first partnership chapter. I plan to continue our normal trips, but it is nice to know we really have a leg up on the competition (unnamed but surely referring to Lindblad – National Geo and such) for joint ventures. And of course, the New York Times Travel trip, in all honesty, Mike, you helped engineer to Portugal and Spain, was a success as well. So, I guess, the question for us in this room is indeed what's next? Mike? Amy?"

Amy spoke first. "As we, Mike and I, have talked and thought about the trip, it certainly for me was a first. Different but memorable in other ways from our own trips. An entire new and important part of the world was opened to me and all those paying passengers, both of AT and RP. In some ways it was a vacation of sorts, in others an education. But my cup of tea is still nature, flora and fauna, and the nuts and bolts of putting it all together on 'International Adventurer.' I want to formally thank this man by my side for coming up with the idea and may I say 'twisting arms' for it to happen." (James laughed at that and nodded 'yes.')

"Mike?"

"Harrumph! Not twisting arms, just whispering sweet nothings in your ears! I still need time for the intense past three weeks to settle in. And thinking back, there were some 'hairy' moments that could have turned out differently than they did. There were no major conflicts or fisticuffs between AT and RP passengers, although there were testy discussions and comparisons. I broke up one in the bar on the Lido deck when AT's old Wonky being his usual wonky self, complained of the exorbitant prices of top shelf scotch on the RP to the bar man and muttered he would be glad to be back on the "International Adventurer." The barman said, "Go ahead, our pleasure, but it's a long swim."

"Add in Odessa for one potentially bad moment, that bus ride from Izmir to Ephesus, and places where local violence could have bubbled up; I'm thinking of Dubrovnik and Crete. And even in the Cyclades and nearby Cyprus. But that makes our trip all the more a resounding success! Bad stuff didn't happen. I tried really hard to present passengers with a blend of humor and seriousness of some pretty complicated history. THE GOK PILES a good example. (Amy interjected, "True, really true.") In the end it was Princess that had set up the itinerary; I guess they had done their homework as well.

"Oh, I know it's too early, but I've got a bee in my bonnet – another idea for a trip, but I think with the 'International Adventurer.' Much more 'traditional.' Vancouver Island, the Inside Passage and Alaska. Right now, it's just one of those 'It came to me moments,' but bears thought."

James laughed and said, "Whoa, Gaherty. Not now, but knowing what you can cook up, 'hold that thought' and someday soon we will talk about it. Okay, I have a busy afternoon and will let you two be off to rest up. Amy, I'm counting on you after some rest to rejoin the IA in coming months. Michael, I'm sure the University of Nebraska will welcome you home. By the way, there is a small 'bonus' for the both of you (he handed us each an envelope), but open it later. Christmas is not far off. Thank you; we shall, as they say, be in touch."

We bade our goodbyes, but not before Amy checked in with Susan and was already talking about rejoining the IA in two weeks, a trip set for the South Pacific and on over to Thailand. She and I planned once again for a day or two in Los Angeles, maybe returning to old haunts like Disneyland or the Getty Museum before heading out. But then came the surprise!

When we woke up the next morning in one of those queen beds in the hotel, Amy was already making us room coffee when I noticed it: the original engagement ring I had bought her before the Spain – Portugal trip of close to ten years ago. She flashed it with her right hand as she served me the coffee and added a delicious kiss. "I'm ready to talk, farm boy."

"Taken aback" is the term; I was taken aback. "So, Amy, what does this mean?"

"You proposed to me once; I accepted. I called it off, selfishly, but am now humbly proposing to you, "Will you marry me?"

Like on the trip and Jack Benny (… I'M THINKING; I'M THINKING …) it took a moment to register, but I said, "Yes, but this time we need to talk and, damn it, be sure."

Amy said, "The last three weeks together, including some serious spooning (as you Nebraska farmers like to say) and love making on board (I haven't reported that yet), but as important, the way you now as a mature man handle yourself, others and life, and me of course, made me think. I can see where I was wrong so many years ago, and like I say, for selfish motives. I am truly sorry but I truly love you and always have. The job was more important than a wonderful man and marriage."

Amy was now in tears, but we were holding each other close, and that evolved to once again, very compatible love making. It was more than the sex this time, it was like, sorry for the cliché, being born again, me knowing she truly did love me. I had always loved her, and the reader knows the anguish, yes, anguish, of years ago. I said,

"Amy, this changes everything doesn't it? We need to talk, to think, and make sure this is for real."

So, sorry, no Disneyland, no J. Paul Getty Museum or Pacific Heights; we spent the entire day ensconced in our room at the Marriott, talking, planning, with practical Amy thinking of the "nuts and bolts" of the future and coming up with a plan. Food was room service, and that evening was room service "fine dining" with champagne and its aftermath.

Amy starting, saying "Geeze, it is now almost turning the calendar to 1990, computers are truly coming into their own, and the infant Internet is on its way. And we've still got the telephone!" Amy's idea, still not with separation from AT but greatly modified, was to work at our future home in Lincoln for research on trip planning and research for on shore excursions of any trips (now limited) for AT. In effect, she would set up her own AT Travel Office. She would go on board only for select trips, perhaps now four a year. And I would accompany her at least twice. She intimated perhaps on that frigid Christmas and Semester break and a bit less frigid Spring Break in March.

I would try to plan my research trips to Brazil and Mexico for the summers and to coordinate with her absences; publish and perish still reigned at the U. of N. on the make to be a "great public university." I might add with a good Latin American Center and a small, but respectable university press. I needed to do some good studies and get them into print.

Would it work? Soon enough we would see.

We set the marriage for June of 1990 in Denver. There would be a church wedding at the downtown Cathedral near her parents' house, the reception and a honeymoon back to Rio de Janeiro. She would fly home after those two weeks to Los Angeles, do a trip for AT and we would make the big move to Lincoln in July and August.

Amy would travel to Lincoln early that year of 1990 and stay with me in my two – bedroom apartment but we would scour the town to find something large for the interim, a four bedroom where we both would have space for my office and research and her very large office, soon to be, AT Travel Office.

There were other issues, both of us now in early 40s. We initially, reluctantly, decided to not try to have children, Amy thinking her clock for that had already perilously come close to running out. We would re-visit the issue many times that first year, but no final, final decision was made. We would look into that maze of the adoption world, but that was yet to come.

ABOUT THE AUTHOR

Mark Curran is a retired professor from Arizona State University where he worked from 1968 to 2011. He taught Spanish and Portuguese and their respective cultures. His research specialty was Brazil and its "popular literature in verse" or the "Literatura de Cordel," and he has published many articles in research reviews and now some fourteen books related to the "Cordel" in Brazil, the United States and Spain. Other books done during retirement are of either an autobiographic nature – "The Farm" or "Coming of Age with the Jesuits" - or reflect classes taught at ASU on Luso-Brazilian Civilization, Latin American Civilization or Spanish Civilization. The latter are in the series "Stories I Told My Students:" books on Brazil, Colombia, Guatemala, Mexico, Portugal and Spain. "Letters from Brazil I, II, III and IV" is an experiment combining reporting and fiction. "A Professor Takes to the Sea I and II" is a chronicle of a retirement adventure with Lindblad Expeditions - National Geographic Explorer. "Rural Odyssey – Living Can Be Dangerous" is "The Farm" largely made fiction. "A Rural Odyssey II – Abilene – Digging Deeper" and "Rural Odyssey III Dreams Fulfilled and Back to Abilene" are a continuation of "Rural Odyssey." "Around Brazil on the 'International Traveler' – A Fictional Panegyric" tells of an expedition in better and happier times in Brazil, but now in fiction. The author presents a continued expedition in fiction "Pre – Columbian Mexico – Plans, Pitfalls and Perils." Yet another is "Portugal and Spain on the 'International Adventurer.'" "The Collection" is a bibliography of primary and secondary works on the "Literatura de Cordel" in Curran's collection.

"The Master of the "Literatura de Cordel" - Leandro Gomes de Barros. A Bilingual Anthology of Selected Works" is a return to the topic of the Dissertation in 1968. "Adventure Travel" in Guatemala – The Maya Heritage" is a return to the A.T. series, the 4th preceded by books on Brazil, Mexico, Portugal and Spain. "Two By Mark J. Curran" combines two shorter narratives on the author's life, "ASU Days" and "The Guitars – A Music Odyssey." "Rural Odyssey IV – Parallels. Abilene, Cowboys and "Cordel" is cultural, historic fiction in the Rural Odyssey Series. "The Writing and Publishing Journey" is a capstone volume and catalogue of all of Curran's books to the present with color images of all the covers and short summaries of the genesis of the books. "Adventure Travel" in Colombia – Moments of Mayhem continues the Adventure Travel Series. And now, "Adventure Travel" – A New Partnership
   The Royal Princess.

Published Books

A Literatura de Cordel. Brasil. 1973

Jorge Amado e a Literatura de Cordel. Brasil. 1981

A Presença de Rodolfo Coelho Cavalcante na Moderna Literatura de Cordel. Brasil. 1987

La Literatura de Cordel – Antología Bilingüe – Español y Portugués. España. 1990

Cuíca de Santo Amaro Poeta-Repórter da Bahia. Brasil. 1991

História do Brasil em Cordel. Brasil. 1998 Cuíca de Santo Amaro – Controvérsia no Cordel. Brasil. 2000

Brazil's Folk-Popular Poetry – "a Literatura de Cordel" – a Bilingual Anthology in English and Portuguese. USA. 2010

The Farm – Growing Up in Abilene, Kansas, in the 1940s and the 1950s. USA. 2010

Retrato do Brasil em Cordel. Brasil. 2011

Coming of Age with the Jesuits. USA. 2012

Peripécias de um Pesquisador "Gringo" no Brasil nos Anos 1960 ou 'A Cata de Cordel" USA. 2012

Adventures of a 'Gringo' Researcher in Brazil in the 1960s or In Search of Cordel. USA. 2012

A Trip to Colombia – Highlights of Its Spanish Colonial Heritage. USA. 2013

Travel, Research and Teaching in Guatemala and Mexico – In Quest of the Pre-Columbian Heritage Volume I – Guatemala. 2013

Volume II – Mexico. USA. 2013

A Portrait of Brazil in the Twentieth Century – The Universe of the "Literatura de Cordel." USA. 2013

Fifty Years of Research on Brazil – A Photographic Journey. USA. 2013

Relembrando - A Velha Literatura de Cordel e a Voz dos Poetas. USA. 2014

Aconteceu no Brasil – Crônicas de um Pesquisador Norte Americano no Brasil II, USA. 2015

It Happened in Brazil – Chronicles of a North American Researcher in Brazil II. USA, 2015

Diário de um Pesquisador Norte-Americano no Brasil III. USA, 2016

Diary of a North American Researcher in Brazil III. USA, 2016

Letters from Brazil. A Cultural-Historical Narrative Made Fiction. USA 2017.

A Professor Takes to the Sea – Learning the Ropes on the National Geographic Explorer. Volume I, "Epic South America" 2013 USA, 2018.

Volume II, 2014 and "Atlantic Odyssey 108" 2016, USA, 2018

Letters from Brazil II – Research, Romance and Dark Days Ahead. USA, 2019.

A Rural Odyssey – Living Can Be Dangerous. USA, 2019.

Letters from Brazil III – From Glad Times to Sad Times. USA, 2019.

A Rural Odyssey II – Abilene – Digging Deeper. USA, 2020

Around Brazil on the "International Traveler" – A Fictional Panegyric, USA, 2020

Pre – Columbian Mexico – Plans Pitfalls and Perils, USA 2020

Portugal and Spain on the 'International Adventurer,' USA, 2021

Rural Odyssey III – Dreams Fulfilled and Back to Abilene, USA, 2021

The Collection. USA, 2021 Letters from Brazil IV. USA, 2021.

The Master of the "Literatura de Cordel" – Leandro Gomes de Barros

A Bilingual Anthology of Selected Works. USA, 2022

Adventure Travel in Guatemala – The Maya Heritage, USA, 2022

Two By Mark J. Curran, USA, 2022

Rural Odyssey IV – Parallels. Abilene, Cowboys and "Cordel," USA, 2023
The Writing and Publishing Journey. USA, 2023.

"Adventure Travel" in Colombia – Moments of Mayhem. Or, Colombia Revisited. USA, 2023.

"Adventure Travel" – A New Partnership

The Royal Princess. USA.

Professor Curran lives in Mesa, Arizona, and spends part of the year in Colorado. He is married to Keah Runshang Curran and they have one daughter Kathleen who lives in Albuquerque, New Mexico, married to teacher Courtney Hinman in 2018. Her documentary film "Greening the Revolution" was presented most recently in the Sonoma Film Festival in California, this after other festivals in Milan, Italy and New York City. Katie was named best female director in the Oaxaca Film Festival in Mexico.